Tales from the
Vienna Woods

Tales from the

Vienna Woods

The Story of JOHANN STRAUSS

By DAVID EWEN

Illustrated by EDGARD CIRLIN

New York: HENRY HOLT AND COMPANY

For Robert

Books by David Ewen

THE UNFINISHED SYMPHONY

FROM BACH TO STRAVINSKY

WINE, WOMEN AND WALTZ

THE MAN WITH THE BATON

COMPOSERS OF TODAY

HEBREW MUSIC

COMPOSERS OF YESTERDAY

TWENTIETH CENTURY COMPOSERS

MEN AND WOMEN WHO MAKE MUSIC

PIONEERS IN MUSIC

LIVING MUSICIANS

MUSIC COMES TO AMERICA

THE BOOK OF MODERN COMPOSERS

DICTATORS OF THE BATON

THE STORY OF GEORGE GERSHWIN

MUSIC FOR THE MILLIONS

TALES FROM THE VIENNA WOODS

In collaboration with Dr. Frederic Ewen

MUSICAL VIENNA

CONTENTS

vii

Contents

Appendices

AUTHOR'S NOTE

SINCE in the first part of this book two Johann Strausses appear—the father and the son—a simple expedient has been adopted to avoid confusion: Throughout Part One, the father is referred to as "Strauss" or "Father Strauss," and the son as "Johann"; after Father Strauss's death this distinction is dropped, and both "Johann" and "Strauss" mean the younger Strauss.

On pages 173-74 the reader will find translations of all café-house names mentioned in the text, as well as the names of certain organizations. Other appendices comprise a complete list of Johann Strauss's works, a list of the best recordings, several pages of extracts from the Strausses' music, and a chronological table showing "The World the Strausses Lived In."

Tales from the Vienna Woods

Memories and Visions

HE HAD HEARD everything his mother had told him a
few hours ago. But it was only now, as he tossed about
in bed, that he realized what it all meant. Earlier, he

had been conscious chiefly of how beautiful her sorrow had made her; had been aware of her small, slanted eyes, brilliant with tears, of the sensitive trembling of her lips, of the slender, exquisite hands, clasped so tightly that the veins stood out. With her hair brushed back to reveal a white brow, she had always had a classically handsome profile. Now, grief touched that delicate face with a radiance that made him adore her.

To what she was saying, he had listened only unconsciously, absorbing her words as a sponge absorbs water. And now, like a sponge, his memory was releasing them. Even now he seemed to hear her soft, sad voice ringing in his ears, as if she were still at his side.

"You are no longer a child, Johann mine. You are a young man of sixteen, and I must talk to you as to a man. You must be brave—must try to understand what I have to tell you." Then, turning her head away so that he might not see her tears, she had said—quite simply and directly—that his father was not going to live with them any more. He had gone, left them forever. And henceforth, he—young Johann—must assume the position of head of the house.

At first, the news had not shocked him much, because he had long been accustomed to his father's absences from the Hirschenhaus, the Strauss family's home. As far back as he could remember, Father Strauss had frequently gone off on long trips; sometimes he would not be seen at home for weeks at a stretch. And even when in Vienna, Father had been practically a stranger to his family; for most of the time he was out at some café-house, either making music there (his regular vocation) or else entertaining his friends. During the few hours that he spent at home late in the forenoon, he would work in his study, where nobody dared disturb him. In recent years, he had been away from his home much more than he was in it.

Johann had always understood these absences, had excused them, was in a certain sense even proud of them. His father was a great and famous musician who could not be expected to follow the everyday rules of life. High-strung, temperamental, moody, he needed freedom of movement just as ordinary people needed food and drink. He lived, for the most part, in a world of his own, the world of music. Even then, Johann was becoming aware of how magnetically music can draw you away from everybody and everything else.

But now, as he lay thinking over what his mother had told him, Johann realized that this time it was different, Father's going away. Before, they had always known that Father would sooner or later come back, to take care of them, to belong to them again, even if only briefly. But now he had left them—forever.

It was almost as if Father were dying. Three years ago, in 1837 it was, he had been very ill. He had just come home from a triumphal tour of European cities, and the hard work, combined with the fatigue of traveling, had seriously affected his health. There were moments, in the long illness that followed, when his life was despaired of. Once Johann was so terrified that he prayed fervently that God would save his father—only to wonder, a moment later, why he had done so, for he was not a religious boy and he had never really loved his father. Then he had suddenly understood: it was not the possibility of losing his father that had so moved him, but rather the realization that, when Father went, with him would go all the wonderful music he was able to bring to people—music seized out of the very air (so it seemed to the boy) and given life and form and heart on an inspired violin.

Now, once again, what grieved him most was not the prospect of losing the man himself. Father Strauss had never been very close to Johann, or to any of the children. Ill-humored, easily irritated by their noise, severely critical of whatever they said or did, he was not the man to inspire love. Moreover, he had set up a household rule that had been gall to Johann: not one of the children was to be allowed to become a musician! And Father had implemented threats with beatings; Johann had experienced both.

But, as he lay thinking, it was not the memory of his father's severity, or even the beatings, that was uppermost in his mind. It had room only for the image of the Father Strauss who was the musician, who had captivated all Vienna with his incomparable music, and who was idolized by sensitive Johann. He recalled Father at work in his study, putting down notes on paper; and the magic moment when Father tucked violin under chin to translate those notes into music so beautiful that Johann, listening, felt as if he could no longer breathe. That these marvelous sounds had been created by his own father—

4

by *that* man, in *that* room (music that, but for his father, would have remained uncreated) remained for him an endless source of wonder and awe.

He remembered, too, the time when he had watched his father in the café-house, playing waltzes with the orchestra he led. Dark-haired, magnetic, drawing from his men and from his own instrument music that soared on eagle's wings, he swept his audiences into delirious enthusiasm. And little Johann was swept with them, nearly bursting with pride.

Memories . . . and visions. For now there arose in him once more his long-cherished dream: he himself would become a musician like his father, a musician who would make his father proud to claim him as son. He, too, would win fame; and his music and his fame would some day bring Father and him together—really together, close, intimate, loving!

And with this exhilarating thought, the themes for a waltz came to him—some wonderful melodies for a buoyant, carefree waltz in the typical Strauss manner. He would write it tomorrow morning . . . and he would dedicate it to his father.

PART ONE

King Johann the First

CHAPTER I

Tales My Mother Told Me

FROM THE TIME he was a child, the tales Johann loved best to hear were not about storybook characters in far-off places. His fairy tales were set in his own city, Vienna; and their hero was his own father. His father's achievements with violin and bow always seemed to him far more wonderful than the most fabulous exploits of kings and princes. When tranquil dusk descended on the Hirschenhaus, announcing the approach of bedtime, Johann would beg his mother to tell him stories about Father. He had heard these tales a thousand times, heard them in all their infinite variations since he was a child

9

in his mother's lap. Yet their magic never seemed to pall. Even now, as a young man of sixteen, these stories continued to feed his imagination.

For example, he liked to hear of the time when his father, then a mere boy, ran away from home so that he might give himself up to music.

Father Strauss, who was born in Vienna in 1804, had been the son of an innkeeper who had died when Strauss was only a year old. Strauss's mother remarried. The stepfather, a kind and sympathetic man, took over the care of the inn and the upbringing of the boy. The inn, called Zum Guten Hirt, was in a crooked, cobblestoned alley in the Viennese suburb of Leopoldstadt. It was a typical Viennese wine tavern—smoky, hot, crowded, noisy, pungent with the smell of new wine—and a favorite gathering place for the locality. It was also a stopping-off place for village people coming down from Linz on the Danube boats. Linz musicians would often visit the inn to make music for the guests, playing *Ländler* and *Teusche* and other Austrian dances. Sometimes the frequenters of the Hirt would raise their voices in lusty singing, or stamp their feet in vigorous peasant dances. And, over in a corner, Strauss would sit unobserved, listening to the music. He felt as if the music were speaking to him alone, and in a personal language which only he understood.

He loved music passionately. His play always consisted in some make-believe form of music-making. He would take two pieces of wood and pretend that they were fiddle and bow. Then, on one of his birthdays, his stepfather gave him a toy violin. With infinite patience, the lad would try to transform its peculiar sounds and squeaks into something resembling a Viennese melody. He and his little violin were thereafter inseparable. He even took it with him to school, keeping it hidden under his desk, and often touching it lovingly as if it were a living pet.

It was this all-consuming love for music, and his determination to devote himself to it, that eventually drove him to run away from home. His mother and stepfather had definitely laid down the law: he must never take up music seriously. Music was only for vagabonds and drifters, and a musical career would bring only suffering, poverty, and the contempt of good citizens. Therefore— no music study for the boy. Instead they apprenticed him to a bookbinder to learn what they considered a useful trade. But how distasteful the work was to a boy with music uppermost in his soul, compelling his every thought! He detested the smell of the glue, the way his fingers got sticky and filthy from handling coarse skins. Besides, try as he would, he could not harness his mind to the job. Always, in spite of good intentions, his thoughts went wandering off into the world of dreams and fancies. He would sing to himself little Viennese melodies, and try to improvise some of his own. Then the stinging words of his employer (sometimes accompanied by the smart of his hand on the boy's cheek) would bring young Strauss back to the reality of bookbinding.

He would tolerate this sort of life no longer. So, early

one morning, with his toy violin under his arm he ran away from the shop. He did not know where he was going, or what he would do; he wanted only to escape from the destiny that marked him for bookbinding! He started roaming along the streets of Leopoldstadt—past Döbling, up to the hill of the Kahlenberg. And there he stretched himself out on the grass, to feast his eyes on the panorama of Vienna stretched below him. The houses snuggling around St. Stephen's Cathedral looked like little chickens crowding around a mother hen. . . . Presently he grew drowsy, and he fell asleep.

He was awakened by a friend of the family named Polischansky, who happened to pass by, noticed him, and was surprised to find him so far from home. Strauss told him firmly that he had run away, and that never again would he go back.

"But why?" Polischansky asked.

"I want to be a musician."

Polischansky, a violinist himself, smiled at the boy's self-assurance and determination.

"If you want to be a musician, you will be one—and no one can stop you. Come—" Polischansky reached for Strauss's hand—"we'll go back to your home and talk things over with your parents. I'm sure we can make them see things our way."

"And no more bookbinding—just music all the time?"

"If it's music you want, you will have it. *I* promise you."

Polischansky was as good as his word. Not only did he induce Strauss's parents to give permission for music lessons, but he himself began teaching the boy the violin. Strauss's bookbinding days were over; he now belonged exclusively to the violin.

Strauss had found his world.

Another of little Johann's favorite stories concerned his father and Josef Lanner, and the carefree, gypsy life they led together as they made Vienna whirl with their music.

When Strauss was fifteen years old, he joined a little band which, directed by Pamer, played popular Viennese music in the cafés and taverns. One of the members was a musician named Josef Lanner. Strauss and Lanner at once took to each other, as opposites so often do. Strauss was full of excited energy and volatile moods; Lanner was placid, gentle, subdued. One had only to look at their faces to see how different they were. Strauss was dark of skin, with intense fiery eyes and a firm, assertive jaw; Lanner was blond, his face rather girlish in its contours, his eyes distant and dreamy. Their two personalities complemented each other, too. But if they were opposites, they also had their common ground: music— Viennese popular music, the music of the people; and on this ground they walked with complete unanimity.

Lanner was three years older than Strauss, but in spirit they were twins, and they became bosom friends. When Lanner left Pamer to organize a small band of his own, Strauss soon joined him. They played at the Wallischen Bierhaus in the Prater section of Vienna; they played at the Zum Goldenen Rebhuhn in the heart of the city. (Here one of the visitors was a round-faced and spectacled little musician named Franz Schubert. A few years later, Schubert was to say that this man Strauss belonged with the immortals!) Their zestful and magnetic performance of Vienna's earthy music found admirers everywhere. Lanner was the poet of this little ensemble: when he put violin to chin, he softened his audience's hearts and filled them with nostalgic yearnings. Strauss was the firebrand; he quickened the pulse and the heartbeat, and made the feet restless. But whether they played sad tunes or gay ones, they echoed Vienna's moods and tempers. In listening to this music, the Viennese found in it something of themselves and their inmost longings and dreams.

More and more the Viennese talked of the wonderful Lanner band, whose music-making set your blood aflame. The inquisitive came to hear for themselves— heard, and were captivated. This Lanner music was irresistible, they said; it was the essence of Vienna. And Lanner became famous.

And how Lanner and Strauss enjoyed this success! Theirs was a happy-go-lucky Bohemian existence in which the two shared equally everything that came their way. We live but once—this was their philosophy; they were determined to make that one life as full of laughter and gaiety as they could. Throughout the length and breadth of Vienna the pair soon became known. Playfully, Vienna nicknamed them the "Blond Head" and the "Black Moor." Their pranks, their little flirtations, their loud-voiced jests were the talk of the town. "Ah, these gay, mad musicians," the Viennese would say admiringly and enviously; "such friendships are made in Heaven!"

Made in Heaven, perhaps; but easily disrupted in a city that breeds gossip and squabbles and feuds. And so it was in Vienna.

As the fame of the Lanner band grew, so did its size. From a quartet it grew into a large orchestra. Then, because the calls for its music grew more insistent, from one orchestra it sprouted into two—one directed by Lanner, the other by Strauss. There were some in Vienna who began to say that the Strauss music was better than Lanner's. What began as a purely objective discussion among a few habitués of the café developed soon into a bitter personal feud between the two musicians themselves. Strauss began to resent bitterly the fact that the music he conducted, and even some of the music he wrote, was in so many different quarters looked upon as Lanner's. Everywhere in Vienna it was Lanner, Lanner—and inwardly Strauss felt he was the equal of his friend. Lanner, in turn, began to suspect that Strauss was trying to usurp his position in Vienna, a position which *he* had won through his own solid merits.

Then, one day, Lanner and Strauss were at the Bock café, drinking and chatting aimlessly as was their custom, when suddenly an innocent word led to one less so. Before either man was fully aware of it, they were embroiled in a quarrel. Resentments and suspicions long pent-up burst out. Word quickly went around to Bock that Lanner and Strauss were coming to blows. On the music platform the musicians took sides and began to fight it out. From there the melee spread to the café itself, and soon the patrons were exchanging hot words and fisticuffs—finally even hurling glasses and chairs. It was civil war!

In this war, the friendship and the artistic partnership of Lanner and Strauss were major casualties. "Blond Head" and "Black Moor" had come to the parting of the ways. Strauss rushed out of the café, blind with fury. For several hours he wandered around aimlessly, vowing to himself that he would show Lanner a thing or two about music; Vienna would soon see for itself whether Lanner was responsible for Strauss's music! Gentle Lanner made no such vows. Instead, he went back to his rooms to write a set of waltzes, *Trennungswalzer* (Separation Waltzes), commemorating the permanent rupture of the two good friends.

Tales like these Johann could listen to endlessly— about Vienna and café-houses and popular music; about mad, irresponsible, and lovable musicians such as his father and Lanner; about the Viennese people who took light things so seriously and serious things so lightly; about waltzes, which contained within them the heart and the soul of all things Viennese. . . . Tales from the Vienna woods, which, to Johann at any rate, made all other childhood stories seem tame by contrast.

CHAPTER II

Vienna, City of My Dreams

THERE IS but one Vienna, but one Imperial City—so runs the refrain of a Viennese popular song.

Vienna, queen city of Europe for several centuries, was indeed incomparable. It had its own beauty, its own personality—both in the woods and mountains of the surrounding countryside and in the city proper with its luxurious baroque palaces.

In the first quarter of the 19th century (the period of the Lanner-Strauss collaboration), Vienna was still encircled by the fortification walls which had been built six centuries earlier. Beyond these walls sprawled the outlying districts, gracious with leafy woods and gentle mountain slopes—some of the most lovable country scenery in all Austria. Here were the charming villages of Döbling, Grinzing, Heiligenstadt, Severing: here, too, the Kahlenberg and the Leopoldsberg. To these villages and outlying places came the Viennese for excursions, to drink new wine (*Heuriger*) in the wine-gardens, to dance, to hear and sing the popular songs so dear to every Viennese heart.

Four gates in the outer fortifications led into the city proper, whose heart was St. Stephen's. Around this cathedral were clustered Vienna's palaces, homes, government buildings, and other churches. Near St. Stephen's were the principal thoroughfares: at the left was Am Graben, a street humming with the movement, the bustle, the idiom of Vienna; across the square stood the Petsäule (Commemoration Column) with its sculptured figures designed by Fischer von Erlach. Am Graben led into the congested Kohlmarkt, another of Vienna's fashionable squares; and beyond that came the Michaelerplatz, site of the famous Burgtheater and of the entrance to the Imperial Palace.

It was a crowded city, with many narrow, ill-paved, and often muddy lanes streaking through it like veins in the human body. Tall white baroque palaces stood next to less impressive apartment houses. Let us look for a moment at the kinds of people who dwelt along these streets and in these buildings.

Society in Vienna early in the 19th century might

have been represented by six concentric circles. The out-
ermost consisted of the masses, while the innermost was
the aristocracy. Between these two were four distinct
circles of society. Just "inside" the circle containing the
masses came the bourgeois shopkeepers and the government officials. Then came the professions—lawyers, doctors, teachers, and the like. Inside of these, again, were
the bankers, financiers, and industrialists. And the circle
adjoining the innermost one included the new nobility
and the more eminent military officers.

The wealthiest of Vienna's aristocracy lived in the
city's imposing palaces. Other titled families occupied the
lower floors of the apartment houses; the higher up in
them one went, the humbler the social class one found,
the attics being tenanted by the poor.

It was a cosmopolitan city. The babel of many different tongues could be heard in its streets: Italian, German, Magyar, Spanish, Bohemian, and Flemish. For
Vienna was a veritable melting pot which attracted to
itself travelers from the East as well as from the South
and West and North. Its market-places were filled with
the wares of the world; and its shops were among the
most sumptuous to be found anywhere.

It was a noisy city—for the Viennese lived much of
their lives in the streets. The clatter of rushing carriages
echoed and re-echoed day and night. People talking,
arguing, driving hard bargains, or merely rushing to and
fro added to the din. In the evenings, the streets often
resounded with music, for serenading was popular. Said

a contemporary journal: "Almost every day, if the weather is fair, you will hear serenades in the streets, and at almost every hour, sometimes even at one o'clock and later. These serenades consist not, as in Spain and Italy, of singing voice accompanied by guitar, mandora, or a similar instrument . . . but of trios, quartets, mostly drawn from the opera and consisting of several voices, and wind instruments, sometimes even of an entire orchestra. . . . Soon you will notice the folk at the windows signaling their approval and asking for encores."

It was a city rich in excitement, color, and exhilaration; sprawling, many-sided, difficult to grasp—like the Empire whose center it was.

It was a city of gracious living. The Viennese had an extraordinary zest for life, because the place itself was zestful. The warm and gentle breeze which descended on the city from the nearby mountains—the *Föhn* it was called—was sensuous, and filled the air of Vienna with intoxication. In the early spring (Carnival season) and in the autumn the spell of the *Föhn* was particularly irresistible. To breathe it in deeply and to allow it to course through one's body was to feel as if one had drunk new wine. It was impossible not to yield to it, and equally impossible not to succumb to the gently self-indulgent way of life that Vienna had long made its specialty.

In the company of friends the Viennese would linger in the café-house over their wine, or their coffee generously topped with whipped cream, and listen to the music being played by the orchestra. The citizen of

Vienna loved good food: tender cuts of *Schnitzel,* roast goose with dumplings, nutcake, tarts rich with fruit. He was devoted to subtle refinement in dress and manner. He adored gossip, since everything that had to do with people interested him. The better forms of entertainment gave him constant pleasure—music and art, ballet, the theater and the opera. The popular music of his native city was immeasurably dear to him. But above everything else he loved the city itself, to him an endless source of exhilaration. For centuries the Viennese had had a word with which he characterized life as lived in the Austrian capital: *Flott*—meaning zest, or buoyancy.

It is true that life was not always gay in Vienna, despite the impression created by familiar plays and operettas. For the city often underwent the kind of political, economic, and social upheavals that inevitably bring hardship, sometimes even tragedy. But through all the fluctuations of fortune that were History's gift to the Imperial City, somehow life always seemed worth living. The Viennese might, at times, lament his fate and curse his luck. But then he would breathe in deeply of the *Föhn,* listen to a waltz, stroll in the beautiful setting of the Prater, visit his favorite café. And he would realize that things, after all, *could* be much worse. However unpleasant existence might be at one time or another, the Viennese knew how to face it, sometimes with a shrug of nonchalance, sometimes with bravado.

> *I stick the sun in my hat,*
> *And play dice with the stars,*

the typical Viennese would cry in gentle self-mockery, quoting a famous couplet by Vienna's beloved dramatist, Ferdinand Raimund.

The grace and charm of Viennese life, its *Gemütlichkeit,* is found in much of Vienna's art—indeed, gives that art its character. The music of Haydn and Schubert is full of *Gemütlichkeit,* particularly their German and Austrian dances, their *Ländler* and waltzes. The same quality appears in the poetry of Grillparzer, and in the paintings of Schwind. It characterized the dancing of Fanny Elssler, one of the most celebrated of ballerinas. But nowhere have these traits of Vienna, or the personality of the city itself, been caught so permanently and so eloquently as in the waltz: the dance that belongs to Vienna alone and in which Vienna expresses itself completely. And by the same token, no one ever interpreted the soul of Vienna more poignantly and authentically than the Waltz Kings who during nearly a century ruled the city graciously and benignly with a violin bow for a scepter.

CHAPTER III

"The Ancient Viennese Folk-Spirit"

AND SO IT CAME ABOUT that Strauss parted from Lanner in 1825, taking with him eleven of Lanner's men; and they began playing in the cafés. At the Zwei Tauben, in the summer of the next year, he brought out his first published work, the *Täuberlwalzer,* waltzes called for the "two doves" of the café's name.

At first slowly, then more and more perceptibly, he began to excite comment. He conducted, and he composed; his *Kettenbrückewalzer* swept Vienna off its feet. His own hot blood seemed to rush into the veins of his music, making it alive and vibrant.

In Vienna, where hardly anything prospered quite so flourishingly as a rivalry or a quarrel—some issue in which one could take sides and fight—there soon arose a "Strauss party" and a "Lanner party." Hotly the Viennese argued and quarreled over the respective gifts of the two musicians. The "Straussians" said that Strauss's music had a magic of its own which no one could duplicate; the "Lannerites" replied loftily that it was nothing more than a good imitation of the genuine article. So it went—Lanner against Strauss, the poet against the firebrand. Vienna, which nursed its feuds, kept the issue alive for several years. And throughout the controversy Strauss became more and more famous. The ranks of the "Straussians" swelled, and the call for his music became more and more insistent.

By 1830 (five years after the break with Lanner) Strauss had almost two hundred musicians in his employ whom he combined into several distinct orchestras. His music could now be heard in many cafés and dance halls, including such fashionable places as the Sperl and the Apollosaal. At Carnival time, he would often direct three or four orchestras in as many different places during one evening, rushing from one to the other to feature some special number.

From every part of the city the Viennese flocked to hear him. And they were bewitched, talking more and more of Strauss. Not that Lanner was forgotten or neglected; he was still very popular. But whereas in 1825 there had been but one musical idol in Vienna, now there were two. Which one you preferred was a matter of personal taste. For languorous and dreamy music you went to Lanner; for passionate, hot-blooded perform-ances you went to Strauss.

"The Strauss waltzes," wrote Heinrich Laub after visiting Vienna in 1833, "are to the Viennese what the Napoleonic victories were to the French. . . . They should erect a statue to him at the Sperl! The father points him out to the child, the Viennese lady to her loved one, the host to his guest.

"What does he look like, this Johann Strauss? The man is as black as a Moor. His hair is curly. His mouth is firm, and his lips curl. He has a snub nose. Typically African, too, is the way he conducts: his limbs no longer belong to him when the desert-storm of his waltz is let loose. His fiddle-bow dances with his arms. The tempo animates his feet. The melody waves champagne glasses in his face. The Devil is abroad! And the Viennese ac-cept this passionate procedure with unparalleled en-thusiasm."

In the same year, 1833, another visitor to Vienna recorded his impressions of Strauss—young Richard Wagner, then nineteen years old, with his dreams of Valhalla, Tristan, and Parsifal still far in the future.

"I shall never forget," wrote Wagner, "the passions bordering on mad fury with which the wonderful Johann Strauss conducted. This *daemon* of the ancient Viennese folk-spirit trembled at the beginning of a new waltz like a python preparing to spring and . . . the ecstasy . . . stimulated that magical first violin to almost dangerous flights."

Clearly the Strauss madness had begun!

Johann was no more than five or six years old when for the first time he heard his father conduct in a café-house. For some time the boy had been begging his mother to take him to one of the cafés where Strauss played. At last, the expedition was planned. Secrecy had to be maintained, for if Father ever got wind of it he would surely put his foot down. Stealthily mother and son made their way to the café and found a seat in a far corner.

Though smoky and noisy, to little Johann's imagination the place was in some sort a fairyland where strange and wonderful things might happen. His eyes drank in all the sights hungrily: the waiters carrying their burdened trays, slipping gracefully along the aisles between tables; the beautifully dressed ladies wielding lace fans; the three stout men near him noisily playing cards. Then a few musicians straggled on to the platform to arrange their music. Others followed. "He'll be here any minute," cried a lady near by—and Johann knew that *he* meant Father.

The noise gradually changed in character as the orchestra assembled. Now it had a sort of feverish quality; the whole café seemed charged with excitement.

Then, suddenly, his father came out and walked to his place in front of the orchestra, violin and bow in hand. Exquisitely dressed, with delicate lace frills framing his wrists, he appeared the personification of elegance. His bow struck sharply on the music stand. A waltz, first slow and leisurely, then growing in passion, rose under that swaying bow. Then there came a passage full of tenderness. Strauss veered, faced his public, and, putting violin under his chin, began to play. His movements, as he played, had a rhythmic poetry, almost as if they were part of the music itself. His dark, handsome face was contracted with tenseness; his eyes were afire. He played on; one seemed to feel that the music coursed out of his body and through his violin, so much of Strauss's own hot blood and heartbeat did it possess. And how his men were magnetized! They played with passion, lifting the music of the waltz to the heights of delirium!

Johann sat and listened, transfigured. He had never before known an experience like this one, sweeping him away as on a tidal wave, carrying him into a new world of beauty. He wanted to cry. He did not know why—for certainly he was not sad, but happier than he had ever been!

Then the waltz was over. The audience shouted its approval. "Ah, surely there is no one like him!" exclaimed the lady near Johann. And Strauss played again—not only waltzes, but also *Ländler* and other Viennese dances.

"So you liked the music?" his mother asked him when they reached home. Johann tried to answer her, but the words would not come. He merely looked at her, his face glowing with happiness. Then he buried his face in her lap and cried.

And for him, from that day on, his father took on heroic stature, became someone to worship, from a distance and in silence. For Johann now knew that his father had such secret powers and magic as are given to few.

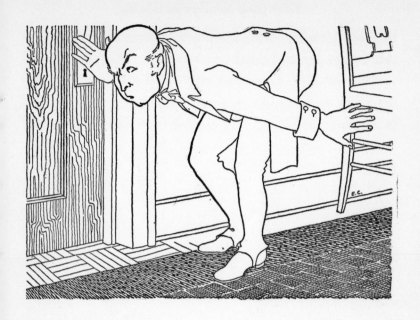

CHAPTER IV

Invitation to the Dance

STRAUSS'S RISE to fame began a new era in Vienna's musical life. The old tradition—a tradition we shall hardly see return—died in 1828 with Franz Schubert. For a hundred years this city on the Danube had been the musical capital of the world. To Vienna, Gluck had come in 1736, and in Vienna he had produced those operas (*Orfeo* and *Alceste*) with which the opera form was to approach the threshold of a new world—the world of Wagner and the music-drama. In Vienna, Haydn had composed the symphonies and quartets which for the first time brought these forms to artistic maturity. Mozart had left Salzburg in 1781 to settle in the Austrian capital, and eleven years later Beethoven transferred his home and his allegiance from Bonn to Vienna. Between them, Mozart and Beethoven had immeasurably enriched every field of music. At their hands, music acquired altogether new expressiveness, eloquence, nobility, so that the art seemed in truth to have been reborn. Schubert, native to Vienna, in his chamber music and his symphonies carried on the torch of Haydn, Mozart, and Beethoven; and in one field—that of song— he created a kingdom of his own. Thus, for a hundred years, the greatest writing in music was done in Vienna, as the city inspired music's creative geniuses.

This was the old era, the old tradition—up to 1828. After that year, and for some fifty years longer, Vienna ceased to be the fountainhead of great music, and became instead the capital of the world of popular music. The Viennese music lover turned more and more to lighter moods, gayer fancies. He who once had idolized Haydn, Mozart, Beethoven, now paid court to the Kapellmeister of the café-house and to the lilting cadence of dance music. The new era, essentially the waltz era, brought new musical gods to Vienna—not those of the opera house and the concert stage, but those of the dance hall and the café.

When in 1830 the young Mendelssohn visited Vienna, only three years had passed since Beethoven's death, but already Felix could regretfully note the musical sterility into which the city had lapsed. In order to sustain the interest and support of the Viennese, orchestras like that of the Gesellschaft der Musikfreunde had to intersperse operatic arias between the movements of symphonies! At the opera, not Gluck and Mozart reigned any longer, but the Italians—the Italians and the comic operas of second-rate composers like Lortzing and Hérold.

The famous Viennese critic Eduard Hanslick recalled many years later: "How petty was the musical life! . . . Lacking any intellectual interests, the Viennese public threw itself eagerly upon the purely entertaining and distracting in art. Not only did the theaters prosper; they formed the chief subject of conversation, and were given the largest space in the newspapers. Having no political press, the Viennese read with incredible seriousness such papers as the *Theaterzeitung* and the *Humorist*. The musical domain was ruled by Italian opera, virtuosity, and the Waltz. Strauss and Lanner were idolized. . . . Today, few can conceive the enthusiastic frenzy which those men aroused in Vienna. But it can readily be understood how much this sweetly lulling dance in three-quarter time did—together with the Italian opera and the worship of virtuosity—to make the Viennese less and less capable of intellectual exertion."

What had come over the citizen of Vienna? Was this a complete change in his character, that he was now given up to gossip and scandal and frivolity?

The answer is partly that the Viennese had always been gay and light-hearted and essentially frivolous; and partly that in the early years of the 19th century this frivolity was intensified by political conditions. Emperor

Francis I of Austria, who ruled until 1835, was an inflexible despot, an absolute monarch whose power was unchecked by any constitution; and his people had none of those freedoms that Americans had had ever since the Revolution. The reign of Francis was a period of repression and tyranny. To help in keeping his subjects in hand, the Emperor had in his employ a veritable army of informers—*Naderers* they were called—who were drawn from the ranks of beggars, waiters, and servants. These spies infested the city, eavesdropping on conversations and reporting to the higher-ups everybody they heard uttering "subversive" political opinions. As a consequence, the Viennese learned caution: they allowed themselves to express only "safe" ideas; they read conservative books that were above suspicion; they went only to plays and entertainments with no political slant.

But all these things were negative. On the positive side, the Viennese were almost compelled to turn to harmless pleasures—to flirting and gossip and dancing. Here they were on safe ground; while they were thus engaged, no informer would be likely to overhear dangerous remarks that he could carry to the Emperor's powerful minister Prince Metternich, and get them into trouble. "So long as the Emperor's spies see us just dancing," they may have thought, "so long as they hear us gossiping and flirting, they'll have precious little to report. So—on with the dance!" And it was thus that their original, native light-heartedness was gradually exaggerated into the frivolity that Hanslick remarked.

No wonder that, when the waltz came into fashion, the Viennese made almost a religion of it. And because they were deeply and essentially musical, they were able to elaborate a light dance form into an art work of originality and real worth.

CHAPTER V

The Waltz: From Meadow to Café

IT WAS from the Austrian countryside that the waltz
came to Vienna. The ancestor of the form was the
Ländler, a slow and sluggish peasant dance in three-
quarter time. A *Ländler* such as the *Prater Tanz am
Wien,* popular in 17th-century Austria, bears enough
resemblance to the waltz to establish definitely the latter's paternity. In the early 18th century peasant musi-

cians used to come in to Vienna by the Danube River boats to play their dance melodies at the suburban inns, and it was these musicians who first popularized the *Ländler* among the Viennese. As danced by aristocratic and gracefully shod feet on Vienna's polished ballroom floors, the *Ländler* became lighter and more buoyant than it had been among the peasants.

The first real Viennese waltz was introduced in Vienna in November 1786 in an opera entitled *Una Cosa rara*. Appearing as the closing number of the second act, it took Vienna by storm. Soon the masses took up the new dance form, and before long it achieved such wide popularity that—according to a contemporary estimate—one person in every four was dancing the waltz. Michael Kelly, the celebrated Irish operatic star who was Mozart's friend, deplored the passion for waltzing that had seized Vienna, particularly at the Carnival balls in the Redoutensaal. "The people of Vienna," he recalled in his memoirs, "had the dance mania. . . . I thought waltzing from ten at night until seven in the morning a continual whirligig."

More and more intoxicating grew the waltz as the years passed. In Vienna, where hearts were light and spirits soared, the people gave themselves up to dancing with abandon. The waltz from *Una Cosa rara* had still been a dignified dance, slow rather than giddy, in the tradition of the peasant *Ländler*. But by the close of the century the form had changed; in such a waltz as *Ach, du lieber Augustin* (still popular today) it had lost its sedateness and become spirited. And the more spirited it became, the more enthusiastically Vienna loved it.

"How potent is the attraction exercised by the waltz!" wrote Count de La Garde upon seeing the dance for the first time. "As soon as the first bars are played expressions brighten, eyes sparkle, bodies are attacked by anticipatory tremors . . . and ecstatic delight breathes from charming faces till fatigue forces the dancers to leave the heavenly regions and gather new strength from the earth."

It was not long before the waltz invaded the café-house. For this was the very core of Vienna's life. Here the Viennese found his social recreation. Here he learned the latest news from those stacks of newspapers and magazines which were an invariable part of the café-house's equipment. Here he listened to the latest gossip, here he heard the newest waltzes. Here, even, he did his work—for many stories are told of Viennese composers, poets, and dramatists who produced masterpieces in the smoky, noisy atmosphere of some café-house.

Each of the more celebrated cafés had its own personality. One was noted for the musicians it attracted— Zum Goldenen Rebhuhn, for example, was the haunt of Beethoven, Lanner, and Schubert; another drew the poets; a third, the politicians; at the fourth you would see most of the Italians living in Vienna. It was a social institution that encouraged comradeship, informality, leisurely living, and it was one of the chief sources of *Gemütlichkeit* in the city's life. It epitomized Vienna; it *was* Vienna.

In another book of mine I have traced briefly the history of the Viennese café-house. "It was in 1683 that the Pole, Joseph Kolschitzky—spy extraordinary to the Emperor Leopold—received, as a reward, the permission to open the first café-house in Vienna. Legend had it that in pursuit of his dangerous duties he had during the Turkish wars been mistaken by the enemy for a Turk and had been hospitably entertained and regaled with a foreign brew. Returning to Vienna, he began to capitalize on his discovery. The defeated Turks left behind them five hundred sacks of a curious dark bean. He prevailed upon the army officers to present him with these sacks. Some time afterwards, Kolschitzky went from house to house carrying a tray of steaming cups of this strange, dark fluid. So great was its popularity that Kolschitzky soon decided to open a tavern, At the Sign of the Blue Bottle.

"Café-houses sprang up in numbers—not without arousing the enmity and opposition of the sorely pressed distillers. Hugelman's, in the middle 18th century, introduced a billiard table; Kramer's in 1778 brought in newspapers and magazines, foreign as well as domestic, for the use of its clientele. By 1815, there were more than seventy-five of these café-houses. They drew the Viennese out of the narrow confines of their homes and made possible that charming . . . expansiveness which according to some is the most gracious quality . . . of the Viennese. The café-house brought *Gemütlichkeit;* and a cup of coffee, or, as some preferred, a glass of this year's wine, made for gracious living, congenial chatter, scandal, or sentimentality."

To the café-houses came small bands of musicians to play the popular dances of the day, and with them came the fabulously popular waltz. One of these small bands was headed by Ignaz Michael Pamer, whose popular music was heard in places like Zur Goldene Birne, the Seitzerhof, and the Sperl. And it was from Pamer's band, as has already been said, that the two young musicians went out to capture the heart of Vienna—Lanner and Johann Strauss.

CHAPTER VI

The Waltz: From Cafe to Ballroom

So EXHILARATING a dance as the waltz, however, was not to be confined to the café-houses and their patrons. It demanded, and it soon received, a more expansive setting. The waltz-dancing disease had reached such proportions that enormous ballrooms arose, as luxurious in their trappings as they were overpowering in size, to provide the waltz with an appropriate home. One of these was the Mondschein Hall, opened in 1806, which amazed Vienna with its glistening glass chandeliers and mirror-like parquet floors. Another was the still more elaborate Sperl, opened in 1807. One year later came the most magnificent dance hall of all, the Apollosaal. With forty-four large drawing-rooms and five enormous ballrooms, it could accommodate more than four thousand people. It staggered the senses of its clientele with its sumptuous equipment: "living shrubberies," "murmurous springs emerging in tumbling cascades," a lake with "real swans on it," "a thousand wax candles glittering from chandeliers," and "a Turkish pavilion in brilliant colors."

Up to 1808, the waltz had been a simple sixteen-bar melody, evenly divided into two eight-bar sections. Hanslick later described it derisively as a *"schwitzender Stubentanz"*—and that is precisely what it was, a sweaty and humdrum dance that belonged to peasants. Yet, in the hands of a few composers like Haydn and Schubert, the waltz revealed its artistic potentialities even within the limited framework of a sixteen-bar melody. It had gaiety, pulse, movement, and infectious spirit.

In 1808, the horizon of the waltz-form was for the first time extended. Hummel, protégé of Mozart and a famous composer and pianist in his own right, was asked to write a waltz to celebrate the opening of the Apollosaal. He wrote not one but ten waltzes, skilfully combining them into one coherent pattern—and the "concert waltz" was born. It was from that moment on to become music not only to be danced to, but to be listened to as well. In other hands, it would later become a symphony of the dance.

In 1819, Karl Maria von Weber further proved the

artistic possibilities of this extended waltz form by writing his now famous and well-loved *Invitation to the Dance* for the piano. Its success was instantaneous, and its buoyant strains were heard throughout Europe. (In 1841, Berlioz orchestrated it, and it has since then become even more familiar in this symphonic dress.)

But it was Josef Lanner who was the first genius of the Viennese waltz. Who can tell?—if Lanner had never lived, we might today not have had a *Blue Danube* or a *Tales from the Vienna Woods!* For it was Lanner who set the form which was soon to be used with such resourcefulness and imagination and genius by the younger Johann Strauss.

Lanner began his career as a composer by writing *Ländler* and other Viennese popular dances, a characteristic example of which is his robust and vigorous *Dornbachländler*. But, fired by the example of Weber's waltz, he began writing some waltzes of his own: his first was his seventh opus, and thereafter he wrote them with inexhaustible imagination. A Lanner waltz (say a gem like *Terpsichorewalzer,* which he composed comparatively early in his career) opened with a stately introduction, in which the main theme of the principal waltz was suggested; this was followed by a series of different waltzes in which one principal melody was consistently repeated; and the work ended with a coda that was a sort of summation of all the themes previously announced, and brought the music to an effective conclusion. But besides establishing a flexible and ingenious mold for the Viennese waltz, Lanner also succeeded in converting a *"schwitzender Stubentanz"* into a thing of rare grace and enchantment. At his best, he wrote with a wide range of emotional expression and with spontaneity and freshness; and he was at his best in a masterpiece like the *Schönbrunnerwalzer*. Some of the most ingratiating qualities of the Viennese waltz—its zest, magnetic attraction, light-heartedness, and intoxication—are to be found in Lanner's waltzes.

But even with Lanner the writing of popular music in general, and waltzes in particular, was pretty much of a casual affair, not to be taken too seriously. Many years later, the second Johann Strauss recorded how Lanner used to work. "Once upon a time it was only necessary for an idea to strike a composer, as the saying goes. Oddly enough, something always did strike one. Those old waltz kings had such confidence in its doing so that often they would announce a new waltz for such and such an evening, of which—on the morning of the appointed day—not one note would yet have been written. In such a case, the orchestra generally betook itself *en bloc* to the composer's lodging, and as soon as he had produced the theme, and a few pages of the piece, everyone would fall to practicing and copying. Meantime the miracle of the inspiration repeated itself, and the second half was composed. Thereupon there would be a rehearsal of the whole, on the spot—the entire business occupying only a few hours. Lanner hardly ever composed anything except in this fashion. When on occasion he fell ill and was unable to write, yet was committed to a piece of music for which no single bar had as yet been written, he would send my father the simple message: 'Strauss, what about an idea?' The same evening, the piece would be given—naturally as Lanner's —to be received with a fresh ovation."

When Strauss took to writing waltzes in his own name he frequently adopted a much more careful and painstaking procedure. His first published work was a set of waltzes, *Täuberlwalzer,* composed about a year after he had freed himself from Lanner. Strauss had learned a valuable lesson from his friend: how to use three-quarter time with variety of mood and contagion of spirit. But to this he was to add a precious lesson from his own experience: that the best effects in a waltz must be worked out carefully and deliberately. In this way, he sounded his own personality and manner. Eventually —with such fully realized gems as the *Donaulieder* and the *Lorelei-Rheinklänge* waltzes—the first Johann Strauss was destined to surpass Lanner's achievements, because his writing was more careful, his effects more studied and planned, and because he combined these with a more daring inventiveness. He was not afraid to avoid Lanner's often too exact symmetry, to inject into his waltzes an unexpected trill, a surprising syncopation. He continually strove for novelty and for excitingly fresh and adventurous ideas. No wonder, then, when he emerged as a waltz king in his own right Vienna found him to be not a duplication of Lanner, but a king in his own realm.

CHAPTER VII

King Johann the First

IN HIS TWENTY-FIRST YEAR, three decisive things happened to Strauss all at once: He broke with Lanner; he started his march to fame by forming his own orchestra; and he got married.

His wife was the daughter of a Viennese innkeeper
—Anna Streim. She was handsome, dark-haired, with
a classic profile. The blood of gypsy ancestry was in her
veins, and she was made of much the same material as
Strauss. She had his intensity and excitability, his inner
strength and force of will. He met her for the first time
when he came with his orchestra to play in her father's
inn, Zum Roten Hahn. She approached to tell him how
much she admired his music, and they responded to
each other electrically. This began a whirlwind courtship, and a few months later they were married.

It was not a happy marriage. It often happens that
when the fires of courtship burn too hotly, they expire
early. Strauss had the temperament of a Bohemian who
refused to be burdened by the responsibilities of a wife
and a home. For so long a time he had come and gone
as whim dictated that marriage could not change his
habits. Sometimes he stayed away from his home for
days without a word of explanation. Just as frequently
he squandered his salary in the café-house, forgetting
that there were pressing bills at home to be met. He
was volatile, hot-tempered, unpredictable. Since Anna
was equally hot-tempered, the collision of two electric
personalities inevitably produced sparks.

All this, thought Anna hopefully, would change when
Strauss became a father. But the coming of their first
child—Johann Strauss, born on October 25, 1825—did
not remedy matters. Strauss was much excited when the
news came that he had a son. He was playing at the
café, and a messenger had come breathless to interrupt

his playing and bring him the tidings. Forgetting cape and hat, he rushed from the café to his home at Zur Goldenen Eule on Lerchenfeldstrasse in the St. Ulrich district. And when he heard the first wails of his son, he exclaimed that this, surely, was music sweeter than any waltz!

But after a few weeks the exhilaration of parenthood passed, and Strauss seemed to chafe more than ever under the responsibilities laid on him. And as he chafed he grew more and more irascible. He did not earn much at the café-house, and he resented Anna's insistent demands for housekeeping money. To him, these calls denoted insufficient appreciation of his talents and his importance; and when she scolded him about the amount of time and money he spent in the cafés when work was over, he retorted that she lacked sympathy with him. A musician, he would cry, needs relaxation, or—as his best friend, Karl Friedrich Hirsch, used to say continually—"a waltz king needs sunshine." A musician should not be expected to worry over watching his money like a shopkeeper. If he is to do his best work, he must have laughter and a light heart; and if a few gulden can buy these for him, it is stupid to be stingy with them! But—he would add bitterly—how could one expect a woman like Anna to understand the soul of an artist?

Then they would quarrel—and Strauss would disappear for days. On his return, he would show penitence and they would make up; but it would not be long before they were quarreling again. It seemed as if a stone wall were rising higher and higher between the two. Strauss wanted his world, the only world in which he was comfortable and happy—music, café-houses, his dear and close friends.

As he grew more famous, basking in the sunshine of the public's idolatry, the contrast between his hours in the café and those he spent at home struck him with even greater force. At the café there was music, wine, applause; at home, only misunderstandings, squabbles, hot words. Nor did it ever seem to occur to him that what he had at home was, after all, largely the consequence of his own bad temper, selfishness, and inability to adapt his Bohemian temperament to the restrictions imposed by marriage and family life.

Certainly, one could not blame Anna for the situation. She was, in her own right, a remarkable woman—sensitive, sympathetic, and self-sacrificing. It was largely owing to her tact and wisdom that, during all these years of strife between her and her husband, she maintained a comparatively peaceful and well-balanced home for the children. They never suspected the depth and extent of her personal suffering. She went about her tasks quiet and resolute, usually with a smile or a song on her lips. Understanding, affectionate, and patient, she rarely spoke a cross word to any of her children. Her overflowing tenderness filled with warmth and security what might have been a bleak and unhappy home. She was forced to play a double role in the household's life, acting as both mother and father. She must provide the children not only with maternal care, but also with the firm guidance, encouragement, and sense of security that are a father's duty. And she seems to have accepted the two roles cheerfully and filled them capably. In all the years when Father Strauss was hardly more than a stranger to them, the children seem to have felt no very profound lack in their lives. Certainly all of them grew up normal and well adjusted.

Anna was a good musician, with sound instincts and tastes. As a matter of fact, she was one of the first in all Vienna to understand and appreciate such composers as Berlioz and Wagner; and at least part of her son's wonderful development as an artist was due to her guidance. It cannot be said that she did not have the acumen with which to understand her husband's music or to recognize his artistic stature. Repeatedly, in speaking to Johann about his father, she explained to the boy what his father was accomplishing, and how. In the early years of her marriage, her criticisms were particularly helpful to Strauss in the writing of his music.

But Strauss was a hard man with whom to live a normal life, and living with him grew increasingly difficult for her, particularly after the babies began to come. Her husband's extravagance and his frequent absences from home made her daily chores doubly burdensome. Besides, she had to exert constant effort to keep from the children her troubles with her husband. This was not easy, for she herself had a combustible nature, and she had to exert great strength of will to keep it in check. But she had will, and that will was strengthened by her love for her children. She could not, of course, keep her fights with Strauss altogether a secret; sometimes the situation got beyond her control; and even when it *was* under control it was often only too obvious. But the ugliness of continual bickering could, she knew, embitter the children's lives and set up in them a disastrous feeling of insecurity; and this she was determined to preserve them from, at any cost to herself.

Strauss's study, separated from the rest of the house, symbolized his own detachment. He had little to do with his children when he was at home, except to make them feel that his authority was not to be questioned. In a good mood, he might pat Johann's head and make some playful remark. But usually he kept strictly to himself, brooking no intrusion on his privacy. When he was working in his study, the house had to be deathly still; at the slightest disturbance he would rush out explosively and give the offender a sound verbal thrashing.

Yet Johann admired his father too highly to be hurt by him. The conquest of Vienna by Strauss's music was now decisive, and there were few anywhere in the city who did not pay him great honor. Wherever Johann went, he heard people whistling *his* father's melodies. *His* father's pictures could be seen in shop windows. *His* father's name was on everyone's lips. Knowing this, Johann was too dazzled by his father's fame to feel any considerable rancor.

And that fame was continually growing, not only in Vienna, but elsewhere as well. In the autumn of 1837, Strauss traveled with his orchestra throughout Germany

—a triumphal march. "That Strauss," said the Germans, "has turned our good citizens into Viennese!" From Germany he took his orchestra to Paris, where his music was heard at the most fashionable balls, including one at the court of King Louis Philippe, and elicited high praise from the eminent composers Auber, Berlioz, Cherubini, and Meyerbeer. Momentarily, such Parisian composers of dance music as Musard and Dufresne were neglected, as the French talked only of Strauss and his wonderful waltzes. After Paris, Strauss went on to London, to play at the festivities held for the coronation of young Queen Victoria; and the eighteen-year-old girl, soon to be crowned queen, had danced delightedly to his waltz music. Evidently, Strauss was not only king in Vienna—he was monarch of all Europe!

And so, though Johann feared his father and went in terror of that mercurial temper, Strauss's presence at home brought the boy not tension but a feeling of genuine pleasure. He liked to feel that somewhere near him his father was writing the wonderful music that made all Europe ecstatic. For hours, he would loiter near the door of Strauss's study, waiting for the moment when his father would begin playing the violin.

One time, his father was busy composing a waltz. Johann stood outside the door, hoping to catch a few strains of the music. He knew that the composition was going slowly and with difficulty, for every few minutes Father would play a phrase on his violin, and then stop abruptly. The boy listened, all ears, as the search went on for some satisfying resolution. At last he could contain himself no longer. Gently he opened the door to the study and walked in softly.

"Herr Vater," he said timidly, going over and striking some chords on the piano, "is this the way you want the waltz to go on?"

Johann had expected a burst of fury, but to his surprise Strauss laughed warmly. "What a monkey you are!" he cried. "You can write *my* waltzes for me, and I will do *your* lessons."

A moment later a mischievous gleam came into his eyes. "You know what I'll do, Johann? I'll follow your advice! Yes, that's the way my waltz should go on. And tonight I'll play it *your* way in the café!"

It was not an altogether unhappy childhood, after all. Such a moment of tenderness on his father's part compensated Johann for the long stretches of aloofness. It warmed him, and the memory of it kept him warm for weeks afterward. At such a time his adoration of his father was blended with an overwhelming love. Rare and brief such moments were—but how precious to Johann because of their very infrequency!

CHAPTER VIII

A Musician is Born

JOHANN COULD not remember the time when he was not profoundly affected by the sound of music. He was conscious of its spell from the time when, as a child in the crib, he would hear his father play. Music was to him, as he grew older, what a story-book or a new game was to other children—an inexhaustibly rich adventure which carried him away to wondrous worlds of fancy.

As a boy, he had no friends to speak of, except perhaps the little girl in the Hirschenhaus to whom he taught the piano for a few pfennigs a lesson, and to whom he sometimes liked to confide his dreams. At school, the boys thought him strange because he was quiet, self-centered, diffident, and entirely uninterested in their diversions. He made no effort to explain himself to them. How could he possibly make them understand what he knew so well—that music was more thrilling than schoolboy pranks and games? And so he preferred to live within himself and his music. Because of music, and the limitless richness it brought him, he never seemed to feel the lack of other pastimes; and because of the warmth of his mother's love, he never felt the need of outside friendships.

In his academic studies he was hardly more than passable; at the Schottengymnasium he was known as a good boy who tried hard and received fair marks. But when once, later in life, he got absorbed in music, all other subjects lost point and meaning. At the technical school where he studied commercial subjects, he was discovered one day scribbling melodies in his notebook. He gave less and less attention to his schoolwork, until finally he was dismissed.

He was six years old when he wrote his first melody. It was during a visit that he and his mother paid to his grandmother at Salmannsdorf, near Vienna. There was an old piano in the house, and it drew him at once. At home, too, there was a piano—but that one was in Father's study and he was not allowed to touch it. Now, therefore, as his mother and grandmother talked busily, he edged toward the instrument, lifted the lid, and began to stroke the keys. And then—almost before he realized it—he was making up a little tune of his own; and it was in three-quarter time.

As soon as his mother heard it, she made him play it over again so that she could write it down on paper. Then she gave it a title—*Erster Gedanke:* her Johann's "First Thought," appropriately expressed in waltz time! How proud he was when he took the manuscript into his hands, with all the lines and notes that his mother had written on it!

From then on, Johann kept trying to think up little waltz tunes. Also, having discovered that he was able to create musical ideas of his own he began to beg for lessons on the violin. But Father Strauss frowned upon any musical activity by his children, and such music as Johann made had to be made surreptitiously. Once, coming home unexpectedly, Father Strauss found Johann at the piano in the study. Down came the whip on the boy's shoulders. "I say you *will* listen to your father," Strauss cried. "I say there must be no more of your silly music!"

Curiously enough, it was not the pain of the whipping that lingered in Johann's memory; what haunted him was the terror of being permanently denied music. Why Father Strauss was so determined to keep his children away from music is not easily understood. He himself was proud of his career, proud of the honors that were paid to him, proud of the adulation of the café-house public. For himself, he could think of no career more glamorous or satisfying. Yet (although this sounds contradictory) at home he sneered at all musicians as vagabonds, parasites, ne'er-do-wells (ironically enough, in exactly the way his stepfather had spoken of them when Strauss himself wanted to become a musician). Such a life was not to be for *his* children. They must become shopkeepers or government officials and lead normal, respectable lives. Some day—he would add —they would be grateful to him for his severity in this direction. But, grateful or not, they must listen to him and obey him now.

Could it be that, in his heart, Father Strauss blamed music and his career for his own inadequacy as father and husband? That he was determined to spare his sons the unhappy home life that he had created for himself? Or was there some mysterious sixth sense warning him that one of his sons was destined to eclipse him in the only world in which Strauss wanted to remain unrivaled?

But it was no more possible to keep a musical child from music than it was to stop the ocean's flow or the wind's flight. Father Strauss might lay down the law, but it was a poor weapon with which to fight the inner compulsions that drove Johann to music. Not lashes of the whip nor the fear of his father's anger could keep Johann away from music. When his father was out, he would slip into the study to play on the piano or on his father's violin. Sometimes he would make believe he was a café-house Kapellmeister. He would line up empty chairs in the parlor, as if for an orchestra. Then he would enter with his father's violin under his arm, and with his bow rap on the chair for attention. Then, singing a waltz, he would simulate directing a full orchestra. And when he finished he bowed to his make-believe audience.

In his pursuit of music, his mother became an ally. Wisely she realized that Johann would know neither peace nor happiness away from music—and her children's happiness was her dearest wish. Together, they mapped out a plan by which Johann might acquire musical training without his father's knowledge. On his fifteenth birthday, she gave Johann a violin. Then she drew a third member into the conspiracy—Amon, a violinist in Father Strauss's orchestra—and Amon, who admired Mother Strauss and had always been fond of Johann, promised to teach the boy secretly.

A café-house musician to the tips of his fingers, Amon taught Johann not only to play the violin, but—equally important for a café Kapellmeister—also to be conscious of his bodily movements and the impression these made upon an audience.

"Look graceful," he would tell Johann; "a violinist must be as graceful as a dancer!"

Amon could be as particular about the way Johann tossed his head, or swept his bow across the strings, as he was about correcting musical errors. And Johann was an apt pupil. With his father as a model ever uppermost in his mind, he would stand in front of a mirror as he played, and try to acquire something of the older man's elegance and courtly manners.

Unhappily, however, after he had been studying for a year with Amon, his secret was discovered. Coming home unexpectedly one afternoon, Father Strauss found Johann facing the mirror and playing a waltz in the best style of a café-house musician. Furious, he snatched the violin from the boy's hands.

"For the last time, I warn you to keep away from music!" he shouted.

At this, Anna hurried in from the next room and, without a word to Father Strauss, took the violin from him and gave it back to Johann. Then—"If the boy *wants* music, he will *have* music," she said, quietly but firmly. "Besides, that violin is *his,* and you have no right to take it away from him."

For a moment the silence was tense. Then Strauss seized his cape and hat and rushed out of the house.

And a few weeks later, Johann learned from his mother that Strauss had left them forever.

PART TWO

Father Against Son

CHAPTER IX

"Good Morning, Son Strauss"

'THOUGH FATHER STRAUSS had abandoned his family permanently and set up a separate home, he did not leave Vienna. To the end of his life, except for his tours, he lived in the city and played in its cafés. But so completely did he wash his hands of his family that he never again saw any of them, even though they lived near by, and he discouraged his friends from bringing him any news about them. He was through with the past!

For young Johann, the loss of his father—terrible though the blow had been for him at first—did not prove altogether a catastrophe. The permanent loss of one whom he had put on a pedestal created a wound that would not soon heal. But it also brought a new gain: the boy was now freed from interference in his pursuit of music. He could henceforth devote himself to it completely. And at once he undertook more serious violin training with Kohlmann, director of the ballet at the Kärntnerthor, and began the study of counterpoint and theory under a well-known Viennese church composer, Josef Drechsler.

In his youth, Drechsler had written popular music. As a matter of fact one of his songs, written for a play by Raimund, had become known throughout Vienna:

Brüderlein fein! Brüderlein fein!
Darfst mir ja nicht böse sein.
Scheint die Sonne noch so schön,
Einmal muss sie untergeh'n.

Sweet little brother! Sweet little brother!
You mustn't be angry with me!
The sun is still shining so brightly—
Alas! how soon it must set!

But Drechsler had outgrown such youthful indiscretions. Now he was a serious musician whose world was that of the symphony and the Mass, rather than of the waltz and the polka, and he strongly disapproved of

Johann's ambition to become a café-house artist. What! a boy with Johann's native gifts devoting his life to making musical truffles!

"You will some day be a great composer, but only if you want to be," Drechsler told him again and again. "You are meant for bigger and nobler things than the café-house. You have real talent, Johann, the kind of talent one meets with only rarely, the kind of talent that can conquer the world. You might even be destined to inherit the crown of Haydn, Mozart, and Beethoven. Ah, that is something to strive for! Why try for anything less? This popular stuff—waltzes, quadrilles, polkas—the things the mob goes crazy about—that's not for you. It's for people without genius! Let's study hard, work hard, try hard—and perhaps we'll make the name of Strauss venerated throughout the world of music—tomorrow as well as today."

Johann would not have been human if he had not been touched by praise and encouragement. But he knew what he wanted, and he was strengthened in his determination by the sound judgment of his mother. No one —not even Drechsler—could divert him from his self-appointed mission.

"You must try to understand me, Herr Professor," Johann would plead. "I don't *want* to write symphonies or Masses. I don't feel them here in my heart. I want to write waltzes, and more waltzes, and make people everywhere dance to my music. And if I have talent, as you say, then I shall bring credit to my father."

"Waltzes, bah!" Drechsler barked. "You'll just be

throwing your genius away on café-house idiots—casting pearls before swine!"

With gay mockery, Johann began singing:

Brüderlein fein! Brüderlein fein!
Darfst mir ja nicht böse sein.

But Drechsler kept on teaching him, in the hope that further study would bring about a change of heart. Besides, it was a rare pleasure to teach a student who loved music so profoundly that lessons became mere play, who learned so quickly that before an explanation could leave the teacher's lips it was already grasped and assimilated.

In addition to applying himself to study, Johann was already composing industriously—waltzes and other dance tunes. He wrote as naturally as he breathed, for that kind of music was in his blood. Sometimes he would show one of his pieces to Drechsler.

"A shame, a shame," Drechsler would mutter under his breath, shaking his huge head, "for genius like yours to be thrown away on café-house idiots! If I were convinced that you are really determined to write waltzes, I wouldn't go on wasting my time teaching you counterpoint!"

When Johann had been studying for a few years with Drechsler—he was now nineteen—he decided that the time had come for his official café-house debut. But before a Viennese musician could get a permit to direct his own orchestra in a café, he had either to be over twenty-one or to have his father's consent; and Johann was unable to meet either requirement. There was a third possibility, however: he might give the authorities such convincing proof of his gifts that they would make an exception in his case. With this hope in mind, therefore, Johann went to Drechsler for a letter of recommendation.

"So you're still set on that idea of yours, are you, young man?"

"More than ever, Herr Drechsler. It's what I've always wanted to do. I think I'm ready to do it, *now.*"

"In that case, there is nothing for me to do but to give you the letter you want—and it will probably be the most glowing letter of recommendation that a potential café-house musician ever earned!"

Johann clasped his teacher's hand. "You won't be ashamed of me, Professor," he returned gratefully, "not even if all I ever become *is* 'a café-house musician.'" Johann's eyes clouded for a moment as he added, "And *he* won't be ashamed of me either."

Drechsler embraced the boy warmly. "You know, Johann," he said, "I *may* be wrong about you after all. I have always believed that genius is a kind of force which carries a musician to his appointed destiny. And who am I to insist that you ought to write symphonies and concertos? Perhaps your own genius is a far wiser guide than a meddling old teacher of counterpoint! Go to your café-house and make your music. And if you don't become the greatest café-house musician in Vienna, I'll thrash you soundly!"

Drechsler's recommendation was thereupon forwarded

to the authorities, together with some of Johann's original compositions and a discreet letter in which Johann promised to include good music as well as waltzes on his programs. Apparently the combination of praise and promise impressed the magistrates, for they granted him a license at once. And Johann promptly set about finding musicians for the orchestra he was to conduct.

Since it was at the Zur Stadt Belgrad inn that Vienna's musicians used to congregate when they were not employed, Johann went there for his men. From the first he worked secretly, to prevent any premature news of his plan from leaking out. The orchestra he gathered consisted of twenty-four men, and he began working hard with them on a large repertory comprising his own music—waltzes, polkas, and quadrilles. Then, with his plans satisfactorily started, he sent his father a respectful note telling him of them. In justification of the step he was about to take, he explained that he had to support his mother and his brothers, and that this was the only method open to him. He was too timid, however, to confess that it was not only economic necessity that drove him—that there was a stronger motive, one that the elder Strauss would surely have understood, having long ago yielded to it himself! But Father Strauss never answered this letter.

CHAPTER X

"A Piece of World History"

FATHER STRAUSS'S friend Hirsch played several roles in the composer's life. He was treasurer of the Strauss orchestra, and its business manager. His nickname— *Lamperlhirsch* (Hirsch of the lamps)—he owed to the fact that it was he who had introduced decorative illumination at the Strauss concerts. But, beyond everything else, he was Strauss's trusted confidant, who could be relied on to lend a sympathetic ear when there was trouble and to do everything he could devise to advance his friend's career. Whenever there was a difficult or disagreeable job to be done, *Lamperlhirsch* did it, especially if it would help Strauss.

And *Lamperlhirsch* now realized, as soon as he learned of young Johann's approaching debut, that here was yet another of the disagreeable jobs that had to be done. As friend, he knew how it would shock and anger the composer to see his authority flouted, to have his son—after all—become a musician. As business manager, he could not but recognize the danger in allowing so formidable a competitor to set up in Vienna. Both loyalty and sound business sense, therefore, dictated that the debut must be prevented—whether by fair means or foul.

Accordingly, Hirsch started going from one café to another, seeking at each one to prevail upon their owners not to engage the new orchestra. And because he had considerable influence, his request carried weight; one after another of the great cafés closed their doors against Johann.

One of them, however, was not to be influenced— Dommayer, of the fashionable Casino at Hietzing. A shrewd businessman, he immediately perceived what a strategic stroke it would be if his restaurant-dance-hall were to be the scene of young Johann Strauss's debut. Vienna, with its love of scandals and rivalries, would storm his doors to hear that concert! Presently, therefore—*Lamperlhirsch* notwithstanding—the city's billboards announced a momentous event:

68

ANNOUNCEMENT

Invitation to a Soirée Dansante

Tuesday, October 15, 1844

AT DOMMAYER'S CASINO IN HIETZING

JOHANN STRAUSS (SON)

will have the honor of directing his own orchestra for the first time, and begs the favor of the public. In addition to various overtures and opera pieces, he will perform

Several of His Own Compositions

Price of tickets—in advance, 30 kronen; at the door, 50 kronen

Begins at 6 o'clock

Soon Vienna was buzzing with excitement. Already well known, of course, was the scandal over the estrangement between son and father; and the forthcoming concert was taken as a sort of challenge by the one to the other. Son against father—Strauss against Strauss! This, surely, was something to talk about. The Strauss-Lanner feud of two decades earlier paled by comparison. A son rising up to threaten his father's hitherto undisputed empire—what audacity!

When the mid-October date arrived, it seemed as if all roads led to Dommayer's. It was an evening of pure magic, the close of a gentle autumnal day caressed by the *Föhn*. Well before the appointed hour of six, the main Vienna boulevards were thronged with carriages on their way to Hietzing. By half-past five, the crowd outside the Casino was so dense that the police had to be called to establish order. Inside, it was not much better. The spacious ballroom was so crowded with tables that one could hardly make one's way among them. "It was more difficult to get a table than a seat in the English House of Lords," reported one Viennese journal. Nervous anticipation pitched voices high, as little else was talked about but the coming debut. What would young Strauss be like? Would he be a credit to the reputation of his wonderful father, or a blot on it? And what was the father's reaction to all this? Would he be here to listen for himself? The voices buzzed excitedly, asking questions, guessing the answers.

Friends and enemies were there—those who prayed for Johann's triumph, those who hoped for a fiasco. At one table sat his mother, apparently calm, but inwardly all thrill and excitement. One of her friends, seated next to her, grasped her hand and held it tightly, for he knew what this evening and its outcome meant to her. At another table could be seen *Lamperlhirsch,* and with him another of Father Strauss's cronies, Tobias Haslinger. Having failed to prevent the debut, *Lamperlhirsch* had come with Haslinger to try to start a disturbance of some kind so as to turn the affair into a fiasco. Father Strauss himself had refused to be present.

At last, Johann leaped nimbly to the platform, and the ballroom buzzed approval. Tall, handsome, elegant, he was truly the son of his father. He was wearing a new waistcoat covered with delicate embroidery, and his hair bespoke the careful hand of a *friseur*. His skin was lighter than his father's, his face gentler and of more sensitive contour. The eyes, too, were less fiery—and more poetic.

Johann raised his bow, and the orchestra began playing the overture to Auber's *La Muette de Portici*. His body swayed and bent with the music; an occasional movement reminded his hearers of the passionate gestures of his father.

"He looks like Strauss and Lanner rolled into one," remarked one.

And his neighbor retorted, "Not a bad collaboration!"

"Now he swings the bow, now he strikes up—one, two, three," reported a Vienna newspaper the next day. "An electric current runs through us, from top to toe. The man sparkles like a galvanic battery, and the cry resounds: 'This is a worthy son of his father!' "

But the crowd was waiting for the real touchstone of any café-house Kapellmeister—a waltz, an original waltz. And Johann complied with *Die Gunstwerber*. It created a furor, and he repeated it three times. People stood on the chairs and shouted. He played another waltz, then still another. *Sinngedichte* (Epigrams) was repeated nineteen times before the audience was satisfied! Then came the *Herzenslust* waltzes and the *Debut* quadrille. And the enthusiasm kept mounting.

Lamperlhirsch looked at Haslinger. Obviously, if they were to foment trouble, it would have to be started soon, or they would be too late. But neither of the men made a move.

Finally Johann struck up one of his father's waltzes—the greatest of them: *Lorelei-Rheinklänge*. It was a sentimental gesture that could not but appeal to the Viennese; and many eyes in the audience filled with tears. At this point, *Lamperlhirsch* and Haslinger rose quickly from their table and made their way toward the platform. But it was not their idea—now—to create trouble. What the two men did was to lift Johann on their shoulders and carry him in triumph through the Casino.

"These Viennese!" wrote Wiest, editor of *The Wanderer*. "Exactly as they were ten years ago. A new waltz player—a piece of world history!" And he added: "Good night, Lanner! Good evening, Father Strauss! Good morning, Son Strauss!"

Late that night, *Lamperlhirsch* made his report to Father Strauss:

"Vienna has found a new waltz king. And, believe me, Johann, he may well become the greatest of them all!"

CHAPTER XI

The Spirit of 1848

IF JOHANN had been hoping that his success would bridge the chasm that had separated him from his father during all these years, he was to be disillusioned. Strauss grew more bitter than ever as—with each passing month —the enthusiastic reports of his son's music reminded him that Johann had defied him; as he realized that his own high station in Vienna's musical life was being usurped—and by his son. He made no move to hear the new orchestra; he refused to perform any of Johann's music; and he defiantly rejected all proffers of reconciliation. "He may bear my name, but he is no son of mine!" Johann's letters were not answered; the emissaries he sent to press for reconciliation were turned away.

The Strauss family accordingly remained divided, and Vienna interpreted the growing rivalry as open warfare. Naturally the city took sides: some favored the son, while others remained faithful to the father; some called Johann's challenge sheer insolence, though others urged that he was but repaying an old score.

Within a short time the two Strausses were, between them, dominating Vienna's musical activity, for Josef Lanner had died in 1843. Father Strauss was heard at the Sperl, the Sieben Kurfürsten, the Grüner Zeisig; "Schani" (as Vienna now affectionately called the son) at cafés no less fashionable—Dommayer's, Zogernitz, Zum Grünen Thore. The father was the leader of a great military band, that of the First Bürger Regiment; the son inherited a post long held by Lanner, bandleader of the Second Bürger Regiment.

Frequently the two bands played at the same time in the same square, hurling their music at each other defiantly, as it seemed, in an electrifying father-and-son competition. The elder man would conduct without so much as a glance toward his son. But the more courteous

Johann, after playing one of his father's waltzes, would bow ceremoniously in the other's direction. "Touching," the younger man's followers called it. "Brazen impudence!" exclaimed the father's admirers.

When, in 1848, the revolutionary movement that was sweeping across Europe reached Vienna and inflamed the Viennese to revolt against a repressive monarchy (the autocratic Emperor Francis having found a worthy successor in Emperor Ferdinand, with his minister Metternich), father and son were on opposite sides of the street barricades.

Father Strauss was fighting for the Imperial interests, and wore the regimental red. One of the marches he wrote at this time (now his most famous single work) was composed in honor of the general who had led the Hapsburg forces in Italy and had conquered Verona— Radetzky. The *Radetzky March* was Strauss's expression of pride and confidence in the Hapsburg rule. Its inflexibly even rhythm spoke for the *status quo;* its formal martial strains glorified the rule of the sword. At a concert in honor of the Imperial regime, the father played his new march before an audience comprising monarchists, nobility, and the higher-ranking officers; and a wave of enthusiasm greeted the work.

Johann, however, was on the side that was fighting to bring about a new order, demanding a constitutional regime and the political rights of the people. His military band now wore the blue of the National Guard. He, too, gave a rousing concert appropriate to the political struggle; playing at the Blaue Flasche such inflammatory pieces as the *Freiheitslieder* waltzes, the *Studentenmarsch,* and the *Schwarz, Rot, und Gold* march. With these he heightened the revolutionary fever of the university students, workers, and bourgeoisie who, here as elsewhere in Europe, were in revolt against autocracy.

The tide of revolution rose to such a point that Metternich, the powerful Chancellor, had to resign and flee to Paris, while the Court had escaped to Olmütz. Father Strauss, now *persona non grata* in Vienna, tactfully decided on a tour of France and England. In Paris he visited the exiled Metternich—both of them bursting into tears at the recollection of Vienna. Before long, the revolutionary tide receded, and a new emperor, Francis Joseph, came to power. Father Strauss now returned to Vienna, to receive a magnificent welcome at his first concert; even the masses seemed to have forgotten the violent conflict that had recently estranged them from their beloved Kapellmeister. As for Johann, his popularity had remained untouched by the late political events, but now he was to suffer for his revolutionary ardor: the new Court frowned on him, and he had to wait many years before his waltzes were played at Court balls (though the Emperor listened to them in private), and before he received the appointment long due to him—that of Director of Music for those balls.

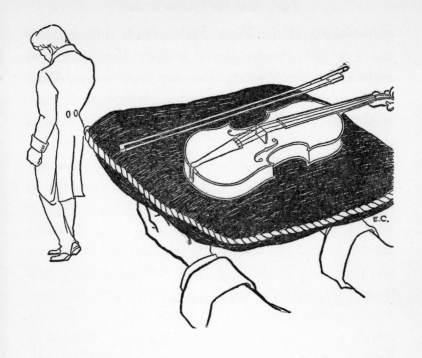

CHAPTER XII

"Good Night, Father Strauss"

AT THE VERY FIRST CONCERT Father Strauss gave in Vienna after his return from Paris in 1849, the bow in his hand snapped and broke as he played. Though the incident attracted little attention, to Strauss himself it seemed a portent, a sign that his career was about to snap. And so the event proved. Three months later he was to direct a concert celebrating the return of Marshal Radetzky to Vienna. On September 21, the day before the concert, while composing a new Radetzky march, he

77

suddenly succumbed to scarlet fever; inflammation of the brain set in immediately. Exhausted by his travels and by the nervous strain to which he had been subjected in recent months, he could offer no resistance; and on September 25, at two o'clock in the morning, he died suddenly.

A messenger went at once to the Hirschenhaus to tell Johann that his father was dead. As Johann was not at home, Anna sent his brother Josef to their father's house. Here Josef found appalling desolation. The place was dirty, upset, and—strangest of all—empty. His father was lying dead on the floor, only half-dressed. It was evident that no one had been near him when he died, and that no one had come in since except the messenger— who had been merely a chance caller who on his arrival had found Strauss dead. Thus died in squalor the man who all his life had been so fastidiously elegant!

The funeral on September 27 was, however, a magnificent tribute to Vienna's dearly loved musician. Thousands watched the procession pass. Three military bands played alternately. Amon marched slowly behind the coffin holding a black cushion with Strauss's violin resting on it. When the Viennese saw the coffin and the violin they gave way to tears. After the impressive funeral services, Strauss was brought to his last resting place, in Döbling. Fittingly, he was buried next to Josef Lanner. . . .

The Viennese poet Bauernfeld mourned Strauss's passing with the following verses:

"Good Night, Father Strauss"

Poor Vienna! Now the gods
Have ceased to love you; they have taken
Your own Strauss, your best-beloved,
*   Your last comfort, and your fame.*

.   .   .   .   .

All that sings rejoicing, springing—
All the harmless, merry laughter—
All we mean by Old Vienna—
*   Now is being borne to rest!*

When, on the night of September 25, *Lamperlhirsch*
came to Johann's café to tell him that his father had just
died, Johann turned his face away and wept.

"Strange that you should cry," *Lamperlhirsch* said
softly, putting his arm around Johann's shoulder. "After
all, he was hardly a father to you."

Johann's answer to this was: "I weep not because my
father has died, but because Vienna has lost her greatest
musician!"

A few days after Strauss's funeral, his orchestra met
at the Sperl to decide its future. Some of the men felt
that, in tribute to Strauss, the orchestra ought to dis-
band permanently. With Strauss dead, it would be a
body without a soul, they argued.

"When he died," said one, "this orchestra died with
him. *We* can go our separate ways and join other orchestras. But the 'Strauss Orchestra' must be buried with
Strauss."

Most of the men agreed. They had always felt a profound admiration for their leader and taken great pride

in the orchestra's prestige. And now they urged that any attempt to keep it together would risk an anticlimax. Let Vienna remember that orchestra at its greatest, under its incomparable Kapellmeister. Besides, who *was* there who could take Strauss's place?

At this point old Amon rose with a suggestion. Young Johann Strauss had offered to incorporate his father's ensemble with his own, thereby keeping alive all its wonderful traditions. Why not accept this offer?

At first, the men protested stormily. Sheer insolence for the son to think that he could overnight replace his father! Not so quickly would they forget that during the last few years their orchestra had played in continuous and bitter rivalry with Johann's; their hostility was still edged with rancor. Did that young upstart believe that he could step so promptly and effortlessly into his father's shoes!

"Please, gentlemen, *please*," begged Amon. "Try to understand young Johann Strauss. He makes his offer not in arrogance but in humility—not out of insolence but out of a deep and abiding respect for his father."

"Respect, indeed!" shouted one of the men contemptuously. "When he can't wait for the earth to cover his father's grave before he wants to take his place!"

"No, gentlemen, you are wrong, all of you. If you only knew Johann as I know him, you would realize how unselfish his gesture is. He has nothing to gain. After all, he has his *own* orchestra, and it is a famous one. After we have disbanded, it is his group that will be known as the Johann Strauss Orchestra. But all he wants is to

keep the *original* Strauss orchestra living. He wants this
because he so greatly admires his father—in spite of all
that has happened—and because he admires us and what
we have been doing!"

Old Amon removed his spectacles and wiped the
moisture from the lenses. "After all," he went on, "it
will still be the Johann Strauss Orchestra, just as it has
been these many years. And, believe me, the boy is the
son of his father. He is a genius. He is the one man in
all Vienna, the only man, who could do justice to our
traditions and our glory!"

The men went on arguing among themselves.
Though some remained adamant, others gradually came
over to Amon's side.

"I *am* right, gentlemen," he kept urging. "The Strauss
Orchestra must *not* die. And it can remain alive only if
Johann takes us over!"

At last Amon won the day. The orchestra accepted
Johann Strauss's offer and permitted itself to be incor-
porated with his organization. The first time that the
younger Strauss directed this new group was on October
11, 1849, at a memorial concert in his father's honor. A
few days later, at the Sofiensaal, the new orchestra under
Johann performed an entire program of the elder
Strauss's works; and—as the *Radetzky March* was
played—a curtain was drawn back, and there on the
stage stood a bust of Strauss. Two weeks after this,
Johann led the orchestra at its first Volksgarten performance.

And Vienna realized that the rift that had for so long divided father and son was now permanently cemented. They were one, at last: father and son—one orchestra, one conductor, one music.

PART THREE

King Johann the Second

E.C.

CHAPTER XIII

"Vienna Will Never Die!"

To AUSTRIA, the most important consequence of that year of revolution—1848—had been that the country was now ruled by a new Hapsburg. On December 2 of that year the Emperor Ferdinand renounced his crown in favor of his eighteen-year-old nephew. Thus opened the reign of Francis Joseph, begun in the storm of a revolution; it was to end some sixty years later in the cataclysm of the First World War. During this long reign he ruled the Austrian empire not always wisely or justly, but according to what he conceived as his duty.

The life of Emperor Francis Joseph was marked by one tragedy after another, all of which he bore with steady courage. First came the realization that his beautiful wife, Elizabeth, did not love him—and never had. Then, in 1867, his brother, the Archduke Maximilian, who had been placed on the Mexican throne, was overthrown and executed. In 1889 the Emperor's only son, Crown Prince Rudolph, shot himself at his hunting lodge at Mayerling because his father had opposed an unwise marriage. Nine years after that, the Empress Elizabeth was stabbed at Geneva, Switzerland, by a deranged Italian. In 1914, Francis Joseph's nephew and heir, the Archduke Francis Ferdinand, was assassinated in Sarajevo, thus precipitating the First World War. And finally the greatest tragedy of all—the realization that came to the Emperor as he lay dying in 1916 that his empire, embroiled in a devastating war, was crumbling in ruins. . . .

But through all these years, as if oblivious of the recurrent tragedy to which the House of Hapsburg was doomed, as if unconscious that the Imperial glory of Austria was dimming to its final black-out, the Viennese kept dancing . . . dancing . . .

"Life is a comedy," said the Viennese. "Vienna will never die," they boasted—and called for another waltz!

Under Francis Joseph, the city of Vienna began to lose its traditional appearance and to change gradually into a beautiful metropolis. In 1857 the old walls and fortifications were torn down in obedience to an Imperial decree, and in their place was constructed a magnificent boulevard known as the Ring. This circular avenue was a beautiful necklace adorning the city—gem-studded with great public parks, handsome buildings, and imposing palaces of various designs and periods. At the north end of the Ring there were built the City Hall, in Gothic style; the Parthenon-like House of Parliament; and the Renaissance structure of the Burgtheater. The baroque Palace acquired new and spacious wings. And, not far away, rose that other baroque masterpiece— the new Court Opera.

All this beauty and majesty and stateliness . . . and within and behind it lurked the germ of deadly decay, decay concealed deep, but through the years working toward the ultimate destruction of the city we call Old Vienna. But the Viennese never suspected it. Perhaps they were too busy dancing—to the waltzes of Johann Strauss.

CHAPTER XIV

Russian Summers

By 1850 Vienna was gripped by a new wave of Strauss madness. The father was now all but forgotten as the Viennese flocked to pay tribute to the son. All the old arguments sounded stale by this time; all the old feuds were dead. Even those who had refused to accept Johann while his father was alive now rallied to him, acclaiming him as peerless. There was no longer any question that he was a greater conductor and composer than his father had been—though how much greater, Vienna was not to realize until some years later.

As a café-house personality, Johann surpassed his father in suavity and poise. His was a poet's face, with soft dark eyes, and black hair clustering above a high brow. A long, waving mustache separated the gracefully arched nose and the sensitive lips. In general appearance, however, he suggested the *boulevardier*. And to his elegant and fastidious dress—frock coat, *dernier cri;* flowing tie; lace-trimmed shirt; tightly fitting trousers—he added an air that stamped him man of the world.

How bewitching the figure that Strauss presented when he stood in front of his orchestra and led his men! Lessons learned as a child from Amon now served him well. His body responded to music as naturally as if it, too, were some sort of musical instrument. It vibrated; it swayed; it bent—yielding gracefully to the rhythmic pulse. His every movement suggested dancing. When he drew his bow across the strings it was with an incomparably majestic sweep. His head and his body and his violin all seemed to be one indivisible organism. He was a sight to dazzle the eye and bewitch the heart. And his music—now sensuous and passionate, now tender and wistful, now speaking with the most delicate accents, now charged with an almost demoniac energy!

Men imitated his dress and his manner, the Straussian mustache being affected by many of Vienna's *galants*.

Women dreamed about him. Even the newspapers addressed him in such raptures as these:

"Your curling black hair with its well-dressed waves . . . Your somber figure stands high above the merry throng. At a poignant passage your bow rises and falls in long, gentle oscillations, followed by your hand, your whole arm; and finally your body swings to and fro from the hips. Then there follows a swifter tempo, the bow makes quick zigzags, springs from left to right, the whole man follows the movement. . . . You are indeed the personification of three-quarter time!"

On Sunday afternoons Strauss was heard in the Volksgarten, where his programs combined good music with popular. Attendance here was something of a weekly ritual for the Viennese, who wore their finest and who came not only to hear but also to see and be seen.

During the week he played at the finest cafés and dance places in Vienna: at Dommayer's on Monday nights; on Wednesdays at the Grüner Zeisig; Thursdays at the Blaue Flasche; Fridays at the English Restaurant in Währing; Saturdays at the Sperl; and at Unger's Casino in Hernals on Sundays.

Whenever a festive affair was scheduled in Vienna— a gala dance, for instance, or a convention of doctors, lawyers, architects, or a ball given by newspaper men or electrical engineers—the demand was always for Strauss, only Strauss. He not only conducted at these events, but he also wrote special pieces in their honor, often with appropriate titles.

In 1851 Strauss toured the principal cities of Germany; and in 1854 began his ten years of happy experiences in Russia.

Certain Russian railway officials, ambitious to increase travel on their lines, decided to make a fashionable resort of the town of Pavlovsk not far from St. Petersburg. But a resort needs music. In 1854, therefore, Johann Strauss was invited to direct a series of concerts, with his own orchestra, in the spacious and beautiful pleasure gardens at Pavlovsk; the contract to start with the summer of 1855.

At the little resort Strauss's music soon attracted the nobility and the rich merchants of St. Petersburg in considerable numbers. It became the fashionable thing to do: you took the train out to Pavlovsk and spent a pleasant evening in the gardens listening to gay Strauss music. Outside, a special train waited to carry you back to the city after the concert was over.

Altogether, the Strauss orchestra spent twelve seasons in Russia, giving concerts from May to September. Though Johann himself did not conduct all of these concerts, he wrote for many of them special music that was enthusiastically received. These Russian summers brought him many interesting experiences—some pleasant, some unpleasant.

An example of the unpleasant sort was the time when he and his orchestra, on their way out of Russia, were mistaken at the border for a dangerous group of Nihilists—the fierce radical element among Russia's revolutionaries of the 19th century. Herded into prison, the musicians had to spend several days there, sleeping on straw-covered floors, living on the most meager of rations, and being ordered around by a stupid government official. They tried hard to convince him that they were innocent Viennese musicians—were, indeed, the famous Strauss orchestra; they even played a waltz for him to prove it! All in vain; both their arguments and their music fell on deaf ears. And it was only when their identity was satisfactorily established through outside influence that he allowed them to proceed toward Vienna.

But the pleasant adventures far outnumbered the disagreeable ones. In Russia, as at home, the great of the land attended the Strauss concerts, paying Johann himself warm homage. The Imperial box was never empty, and some of the Petersburgers called on him at his villa to meet him personally.

The public, too, seemed never to tire of him and his music. The concerts sometimes lasted as long as five hours, yet even at that the audience proved insatiable. On one occasion—an evening concert—his hearers were particularly appreciative, responding zestfully to number after number. When the stated program was over, they refused to leave the hall. They shouted and stamped, demanding more music. In vain the railway officials blew their warning whistles, even coming into the hall to say that the St. Petersburg train would leave without them if they did not board it at once. Still they didn't budge. The train sounded its piercing whistle several times;

then it actually did leave the station—and there was not another train for the city till morning!

With a broad and appreciative grin, Johann resumed his position at the stand. "Well, you didn't want to leave *us*," he told the audience; "and now it is we who refuse to leave *you!*" He then proceeded to direct an entire additional concert, through half the night, until—limp with fatigue—neither he nor his men could play another bar.

In Russia, too, Johann fell in love—seriously, for the first time. Olga Smirnitzki was the daughter of an aristocrat. Young, attractive, sentimental, fond of good books, art, and music, she saw in Strauss the realization of all her romantic dreams. Her father, however, disapproved. His daughter marry a Viennese café-house musician?—Never! Thus Johann and Olga had to arrange clandestine meetings in the best romantic tradition; they exchanged tender *billets-doux* hidden in boxes of bonbons and transmitted through sympathetic friends. Olga's father, knowing that the affair was still going on, worked stubbornly to break it up. As for Strauss's side of it, his mother was equally opposed to the match, fearing that it would prove none too happy for either party.

Eventually, after several months, separation began to do what neither parent had been able to effect. Johann, back at home in Vienna, wrote less and less ardently to his beloved. The letters from St. Petersburg, too, grew less frequent and less passionate. Then the correspondence stopped altogether. Neither lover mourned the end of an affair which, truth to tell, had become a good deal of a bore. Olga eventually married in her own world; and Johann nostalgically memorialized his Russian raptures in a new series of dance melodies!

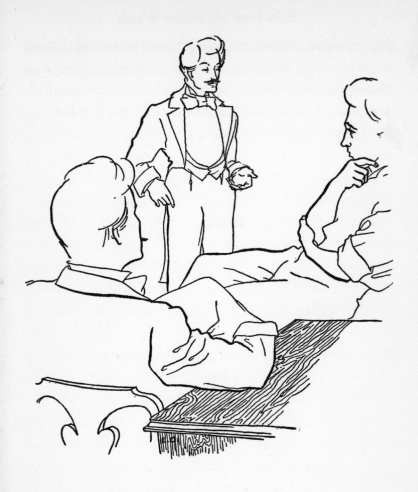

CHAPTER XV

Strauss Blood is Musical Blood

THE CALL for Strauss music was growing so insistent, both in Austria and elsewhere, that Johann realized he must soon get help if he was to carry on and fill all the important engagements that were coming his way. Dur-

95

ing the early 1850's he began to suffer increasingly from overwork, and badly needed a rest. Besides, he wanted more time for composing; the creative urge was pressing him hard. He therefore looked around for someone to act as deputy orchestra director—somebody who could take his place during his absences from Vienna. And he found this deputy in his own house: his brother Josef.

The younger by two years, Josef had been an architecture student and gave promise of success as an inventor. But—with Strauss blood flowing in his veins—he was naturally musical as well. But he was hardly cut out for the café-house. With his austere and brooding expression, he looked more like a clergyman than an orchestra conductor. Sensitive and idealistic, he approached everything with serious purpose and high integrity. As a boy he had been intended by his father for the army; but he had said firmly, "I will not learn to kill men!" He preferred working for their good instead, and was bent on a scientific career. Popular music and the café-house he regarded somewhat contemptuously as the idle pastimes of frivolous people. Though he had no desire to devote himself to music, if ever he did he would aim at higher kinds! He worshipped Beethoven, the *Eroica* Symphony being a prime favorite with him. At first, therefore, he turned deaf ears to Johann's suggestion that he become a café-house musician.

But Johann was both stubborn and persuasive. He needed help, and no one but a Strauss must lead the Strauss orchestra! Besides, Josef had a real bent for music, and if he were to put his mind to it he could bring added glory to the Strauss name.

"If you want to become a scientist some day," Johann pleaded, "I won't stand in your way. All I'm asking is that you help me out *now*—temporarily—while I am tired and needing a rest. Later on, you can go back to your laboratory, and with my blessing!"

Mother Strauss did her part to overcome Josef's reluctance, and with the same argument that Johann had used. "No one but a Strauss must lead the orchestra," she urged. "If from time to time Johann is unable to conduct his men, then either they must be led by you, Josef —or they won't play at all!"

So Josef yielded at last. He would try it, he said. And what Josef tried, he usually did well. To prepare himself for the new job, he began to study music seriously; and he studied with the same passion and concentration that he applied to everything else. It was in 1853 that he wrote his first waltz—and it was a good one. It was in the same year that he took his brother's place for the first time, giving a creditable performance. Josef directed not with violin and bow, as Johann did, but with a baton. He had a gift for conducting, and something of his passionate zeal carried over to his men. He discovered that he really liked the work—enjoyed leading the men in playing with fire and spirit, enjoyed feeling the music course and flow through his swaying baton. And he could write waltzes—supple, heart-warming waltzes. Eventually he was to produce such waltz masterpieces as *Delirienwalzer, Sphärenklängenwalzer,*

Dorfschwalbenwalzer, and *Aquarellenwalzer,* which proved that he was a Strauss in more than name.

Yes, Strauss blood was musical blood! Now that Josef had yielded himself to musical activity, there was no more talk of his becoming a scientist!

Eventually there was a third Strauss, as well, conducting the Strauss orchestra. Eduard, ten years younger than Johann, was a strikingly handsome boy. Though "Edi" had set his heart on becoming a writer, he did not require much persuasion to turn Kapellmeister instead. Indeed, from his boyhood on, he had had a high regard for waltz music and the café-house and had secretly nursed the wish to emulate his famous brother.

Eduard conducted his first concert in 1859. Thereafter, for fifty years, he continued to conduct and to write. Although he did not possess either Johann's genius or Josef's talent, he was nevertheless a competent musician. He had his own considerable following—though it must be confessed, owing rather to his strikingly Adonislike appearance than to his music. The women of Vienna adored him. And there was one period when he allowed his success to turn his head, quarreling with Johann because he insisted on his own way with the orchestra and its policies. Actually (though he would not admit it even to himself) he was fighting against the destiny that forced him always to play second fiddle to Johann. Not even the diplomacy of Mother Strauss could avert a temporary rupture between the two brothers. But they were soon reconciled: Johann had no wish to repeat the tragic history of his father and himself. Often, indeed, he even emphasized Eduard's popularity by laughingly referring to himself as "Strauss—you know: Edi's brother!"

Despite occasional misunderstandings and disagreements, then, the three brothers worked together harmoniously. With Josef, and later Eduard, relieving him competently, Johann was able to relax his activities without any sacrifice of prestige or popularity for the various Strauss orchestras. The three took turns in directing these. Sometimes, as in the Sofiensaal, they appeared simultaneously, each leading a different ensemble! They even composed pieces in collaboration—token of the unanimity of their creative thinking, in spite of their diverse temperaments. Together, Johann and Josef wrote the famous *Pizzicato Polka,* as well as the *Monstrequadrille* and the *Vaterländischer Marsch;* and Johann, Josef, and Eduard composed the *Schützenquadrille* and the *Trifolienwalzer.*

CHAPTER XVI

"You Are My Destiny"

IN THE SALONS of Vienna, Henrietta Treffz was famous. She had once been a fine opera singer. Felix Mendelssohn had dedicated songs to her; Berlioz had praised her warmly; and her contemporaries often compared her to Jenny Lind. But this had been twenty years earlier, and by the 1860's the memory of these triumphs had grown dim. If the Viennese now honored Henrietta Treffz it was not for what she had been years ago but for what she was at that very hour. To a striking beauty, now grown soft and delicate in maturity, she added fine intelligence, sound judgment, keen awareness, and considerable knowledge of music. She was definitely a *person;* one was fascinated by her beauty and carriage, and stimulated by her keen mind and sound opinions. She dominated Vienna's salons, and—perhaps her greatest charm—she did it effortlessly, unconsciously, with quiet and unassuming modesty.

It was at the salon of her good friend Baron Moritz Tedesco that Johann Strauss met Henrietta. He had been attracted to women before; in Russia, as we have seen, he had fallen in love with Olga Smirnitzki. But his feeling for Henrietta was a new experience. Almost at once, he was captured by her completely. Johann, now in his middle thirties, could appreciate her maturity and innate wisdom. Compared with Henrietta, Olga had been a naïve schoolgirl. No need, now, for clandestine meetings, for love-notes hidden among chocolates, to stimulate romance. Henrietta *was* romance—with her ripe charm, her scintillating air, her alert mind, her delicacy and refinement, her vernal freshness of spirit. To be with her, Johann felt, was to be young and mature all at once; to forget time; to exist in a perpetual state of mild intoxication. A few meetings with her, and she became the center of his world. The music he now wrote was written for her. His one compelling goal now was to please her, to excite and intrigue her just as she excited and intrigued him. In short, Johann was profoundly in love, and the knowledge that she also loved him made him glow.

It was on a summer evening in 1862, during a leisurely stroll in the Prater, that Johann asked Henrietta if she would marry him.

"Tomorrow, if you want, Schani darling," she replied gayly. "Nothing in the world would make me happier and prouder than to be Frau Strauss!"

They decided to marry as soon, and as secretly, as possible. Both realized that Vienna would expect a ceremony hardly short of royal; but they felt that their love was something too personal and intimate to be displayed publicly and with such pomp.

Only a few friends, therefore, together with Johann's family, were present when he and Henrietta were married at St. Stephen's Cathedral on August 27. And when, some time later, the Viennese learned the news, they were certainly caught unawares, so secretly had the arrangements been planned and carried out!

Henrietta now became the second woman to influence and dominate Johann's life. The first, of course, had been his mother, who had helped to start him on his café-house career and had then guided him skillfully toward his present success in it. Now, another woman was to take his mother's place. And Mother Strauss knew this. A few days after the marriage she went to the new apartment on the Praterstrasse and turned over to Henrietta all of Johann's money that she had saved for him from his earnings during the past two decades. It came to a great deal of money—really a fortune. But what touched Henrietta was not the amount, but its significance: she recognized it as a symbol, knew that Mother Strauss in passing it on was yielding up her command of Johann's life—making way for her son's bride.

And Henrietta was undeniably capable of taking over the role until now held by Johann's mother. An artist herself, Henrietta not only understood Johann's art, but realized—perhaps even more clearly than Johann himself—that it might, if properly directed, lift him to still higher levels of achievement. Gifted with a fine intuition, she was companion and friend as well as wife; competent in household management, she knew how to establish for him, at last, a peaceful and comfortable life. She was indeed—in the words of a waltz he was to write later—"his destiny."

For her, Johann built a beautiful villa in Hietzing, not far from Schönbrunn where the Imperial Palace was, and fitted it out luxuriously. One of the rooms in the villa Henrietta furnished as a sanctuary for Johann where he might work undisturbed. "This," she told him proudly, "is your 'palace'!"

He knew what she meant. Henrietta had faith in Johann's genius and wanted him to do much more composing, much less conducting. And he yielded to her wish; Henrietta's desires were not easily to be denied. His appearances in the café now became rarer, as more and more his brothers Josef and Eduard took his place and filled his engagements; only for special performances, and then only at intervals, did he make a personal appearance. Instead, he buried himself in his workroom in Hietzing and composed steadily, frequently late into the night. He worked more painstakingly than ever before; not for him now that business of scratching out a waltz in a few minutes with hurried strokes of the pen. For the first time he had leisure to concern himself with details, with little nuances; he planned his effects; he slaved over his contrasts. Haste gave way to the true artist's care for the details that count.

His love for Henrietta, and his inordinate desire to please her, seemed to tap hidden springs within him. His inspiration gushed forth as never before. Under her influence he grew mature, his art deeper and richer; the early unrest was replaced by a profound and serene fertility.

He began writing a new kind of waltzes, conceived so musically and with such a wealth of invention that they have been called "symphonies for dancing."

New waltzes like *Morgenblätter* (Morning Journals). . . . When the French genius of opéra-comique, Jacques Offenbach, came to Vienna in 1864, he was invited by the Press Club "Concordia" to compose a waltz for its use; and he wrote *Abendblätter* (Evening Journals). The club asked Johann, too, for a waltz. As though to emphasize the rivalry between Offenbach and himself, he named his the *Morgenblätter* waltz. For weeks Vienna argued over which work was the better; but, although Offenbach's was then more generally given the palm, today that waltz is forgotten, while Strauss's has proved to be immortal.

Or *new* waltzes like the wonderful *Tales from the Vienna Woods.* . . . In writing this gem, in which all the enchantment and magic of Old Vienna seems to have been captured permanently and unforgettably, Strauss was inspired by the idea of the tired city-worker, chained to a desk all week, but on Sunday escaping to the Vienna woods for relaxation and freedom. To the Viennese, the Vienna woods meant open spaces and liberation from the weary tasks of the week.

Or still other *new* waltzes—how seemingly endless the flow in which they now poured forth! *Artists' Life* . . . *Wine, Woman, and Song* . . . *A Thousand and One Nights.* . . .

Or, most famous of all, a *new* waltz like *The Beautiful Blue Danube.* . . .

CHAPTER XVII

The Beautiful Blue Danube

THE RIVER DANUBE, which rises at Donaueschingen in Germany's Black Forest and flows for 1,750 miles before it empties into the Black Sea, has several distinctive attributes. In the first place it leads European rivers in point of volume; it is the only great European river to run eastward; and it is one of the few that are outstanding for rich historical associations.

But there is one thing that the Danube is *not*. It is not blue—at least, as it flows past Vienna. It sometimes has a murky gray color, sometimes a rather sickly green. But

106

the sentimental Viennese, so prone to glorify anything connected with their city, have long regarded it as brilliant blue—and beautiful! One of the earliest references to its "blue" is found in a poem by Karl Beck, who lived in Vienna from 1848 onward:

> *Und ich sah dich reich an Schmerzen,*
> *Und ich sah dich jung und hold. . . .*
> *An der Donau, an der schönen blauen Donau!*
>
> *And I saw thee rich in sorrow,*
> *And I saw thee young and fair. . . .*
> *By the Danube, by the beautiful Blue Danube!*

Johann Strauss, too, along with all his fellow-Viennese, thought of the river as blue, and it was this idea of his that gave birth to his most famous waltz.

Late in 1866 the director of the Vienna Men's Singing Society, Johann Herbeck, asked Strauss to compose a choral waltz for that organization. Strauss had never before written for voice, but Henrietta—who loved vocal music—begged him to consent. At once he decided to set to music Karl Beck's familiar paean to Vienna and its river. On completing *The Beautiful Blue Danube* he sold it to the publisher Spina for 150 gulden (about $75). And on February 15, 1867, it was introduced at the Dianasaal by the Men's Singing Society and the Strauss orchestra.

Like every new Strauss waltz it was received warmly. But it would be an exaggeration to say that this finest and most famous of all Strauss waltzes—the one piece of music which, more than any other, has spread the name of Vienna and its river to the furthest parts of the globe—created a sensation at its birth. As a matter of fact, the *Blue Danube* waltz did not start on its way toward world fame for some months later, and this was not in Vienna, but in Paris.

In the spring of 1867 Strauss was invited to direct a few concerts at the grandiose International Exhibition in Paris. Princess Metternich arranged a special ball in his honor on May 28 at the Austrian Embassy. At this ball Strauss conducted the orchestra, and one of the numbers played was *The Blue Danube*. Perhaps the music aroused nostalgic recollections among the Viennese living at the Embassy; or perhaps they were astute enough to realize that in this work, "the City of Dreams" had once and for all found its musical glorification. In any case, the Paris première was a notable triumph. From the Emperor and Eugénie down, the brilliant audience gave the new work thunderous acclaim. The American wife of the Danish minister, Mme. de Hegermann-Lindencrone, wrote home to her mother the next day: "No one thought of dancing; everyone wanted to listen to the waltz. And how Strauss played it! With what fire and *entrain!* We had thought Waldteufel perfect; but when you heard Strauss you said to yourself you had never heard a waltz before."

At once Johann was the sensation of the Paris social season. No function was truly successful if he did not participate; no festivity worthy of note unless his music was presented. The Paris newspapers "wrote him up" day after day—"he has the devil in his body," declared one of them.

With Strauss's striking success in Paris came also recognition and praise for *The Blue Danube*. Everywhere in Paris it was played. And it was a question which one had won the heart of Paris more completely: the composer or his waltz.

The popularity of *The Blue Danube* next spread to England; Strauss himself introduced it at Covent Garden in London. And from England it gradually started on its way around the globe. Copies of the printed score were demanded in far-off cities of Australia and Asia. Spina, who on publishing it had had no great hope that it would be successful, was presently so deluged by orders that he had to have a hundred new copper plates made from which to print a million copies.

No figures are available on how many copies of *The Blue Danube* have been sold since 1867, though such figures would undoubtedly prove it to have been the greatest "song hit" of all time. We need no figures, however, to assure us that this is one of the best-loved popular works in musical history. Its melodies refuse to die; it is music that has penetrated into the remotest corners of the civilized world—music that people of many countries have sung and danced to for more than two generations, and will go on singing and dancing to for many generations to come.

CHAPTER XVIII

Vienna Blood

JOHANN STRAUSS often said that it was his ambition to write waltzes intended not for dancing but for hearing—music of such intrinsic originality that, besides being waltzed to, it could be taken out of the dance hall and played on the concert stage even more effectively.

That he realized this ambition, and realized it completely, is the reason why he belongs with the immortals. Strauss's world is not the world of Bach and Beethoven; it is more restricted and on a less lofty level. But in that world Strauss is as peerless as Bach and Beethoven were in theirs. We do not condemn a meadow for not being an Alpine peak; each has its peculiar beauty and charm for us. So with a Johann Strauss waltz; it has its own place in the scheme of art.

The great men of music have always appreciated this truth. The conductor Hans von Bülow used to say that a Strauss waltz is important music, belonging in the symphony hall. Johannes Brahms, in autographing Henrietta's fan with the first bars of *The Blue Danube,* wrote below the music: "Not by me—unfortunately!" When Wagner was at the height of his creative powers, he asked his favorite conductor, Anton Seidl, to play some Strauss waltzes for him. On hearing *Wine, Woman, and Song,* Wagner was so captivated by it at one point that he seized the baton from Seidl's hand and himself conducted the rest of the piece! And Offenbach, Verdi, Delibes, Goldmark, Gounod—all these were among the celebrated musicians who revered Strauss, regarding him very much as their equal.

For, although Strauss wrote popular music—dance music—his work often bears the hallmark of greatness. Much of it is deathless, as fresh and cogent today, in a completely changed setting, as it was years ago in its original *milieu.* In his hands the waltz-form acquired new stature and dimensions. With him the final step was taken in the revolution begun with Lanner and continued with Father Strauss. He explored and enriched all the artistic potentialities of the form; and, since his time, no one has been able to carry these further. As Paul Bechert wrote: "He elevated the waltz to a stage where it could not be improved upon. By him, the originally simple form was developed into a thing of subtle art. It was no longer merely three-quarter rhythm supported by simple broken chords in the bass and given melodic treatment: he made it a vehicle for expressing diverse moods of the widest variety. Just as Schubert created the *Lied* out of the simple and rudimentary folk song, so

Strauss made of the waltz an art-form in the highest sense."

Strauss had always had fertility of ideas—fetching ideas that seduce and enchant. Now, at thirty-seven—in 1862, the year of his marriage to Henrietta—he was to achieve the proper dress for these ideas. He was at last producing work that embodied his love of Vienna and his gratitude for all that the city had given him: inspiration to creative work, a copious reservoir of ideas, popularity and fame, his wonderful home at Schönbrunn, and Henrietta! His harmonies became richer, his changes of pace more pulse-quickening, his instrumentation more exquisite. His effects in rhythm and harmony were sometimes so daring that critics branded him a "futurist."

He was acquiring symphonic breadth as well. Some of the elaborate introductions to his waltzes (to *Wine, Woman, and Song, Tales from the Vienna Woods,* and *Roses from the South,* for example) are symphonic preambles to the dances themselves, combining compositorial skill with inexhaustible musical inventiveness. And many a coda, in which he sums up the principal thematic material of the entire piece, is of highly ingenious contrapuntal texture; that of *Artists' Life* is as skillfully woven as a rich tapestry. Finally—between introduction and coda—there is the parade of waltz melodies, now supple and full of grace, and now endowed with a peasant heaviness; here poignant and nostalgic, there as effervescent as champagne. Moods and atmospheres of the utmost enchantment are evoked. The scene continually changes, ever full of surprise and variety; for Strauss knew how to paint many different pictures with the same brush, and from the same palette.

In achieving the familiar Straussian enchantment, he developed a method that no one since his time has been able to duplicate: a way of casually dropping on the melodic line a trill or a mordent—like a precious gem—giving it new grace and charm; or taking the mere seed of an idea and bringing it slowly yet inevitably into full flower (as in the *Blue Danube* waltzes, the chief one of which is developed out of the simple opening D-major triad); of prefacing a waltz, that is to soar, with a brief passage of brooding introspection; of using crescendi and ritardandi with magnetic effect; of sprinkling staccati over his pages like so much stardust; of achieving flippant, almost impudent, attitudes with fleeting grace notes; of conveying an irresistibly piquant wit through an accelerando passage. . . .

Not only is Strauss music great music in its own genre—it is uniquely Viennese music. The city and its people are there—the froth and gaiety and love of life, and some of the inner unrest and struggle as well. If we knew nothing of 19th-century Vienna beyond these waltzes, we should still be able to get from them a fairly accurate conception of the city.

Lanner and Father Strauss, too, had had Vienna blood in their music. But Johann went further: he caught the city's heart and soul as well. Whatever history may yet have in store for the Viennese, their city can never die so long as the Strauss waltzes live. For the Strauss waltzes are—Vienna.

CHAPTER XIX

Death Takes the Two Dearest

LIFE HAD BEEN GOOD to Johann. It had given him both a great talent and the career in which to exercise it. It had given him fame and recognition from the very first without forcing him to taste the bitter potion of struggle, frustration, and despair. It had brought him two noble women to steer him safely towards his artistic destiny: his mother, and his wife Henrietta. Little had been denied him. Truly he traveled under a kindly star!

But it was hardly to be expected that, kind though life had been, it should spare him entirely from tragic hours. Two such experiences befell almost simultaneously, both in 1870. On February 18, Josef found their mother asleep in her chair, her head resting against the back; at least, he thought she was sleeping—actually she was dead, having passed out of life quietly, no one could tell exactly when.

Her death struck Johann such a bitter blow that he could not attend her funeral; he feared that, if he were to go, he would collapse. He therefore stayed at home, alone with his sorrow. Let idle and malicious tongues gossip, if they wished, about his refusal to witness his mother's burial; his closest friends would understand and sympathize—just as his mother certainly would have.

Along with his grief, Johann could not help feeling a certain measure of guilt. He did not try to deceive himself: his mother had not been happy during her last years, and in a sense this had been his fault. Henrietta had taken his mother's place in his life, so that Anna no longer came first. No longer did he look to her for advice and criticism and help—it was Henrietta who now supplied these. Not that Mother Strauss had ever blamed either of them, being wise enough to recognize the situation as a normal one; but it had hurt her, none the less, to lose her unique status with her eldest son. The only way in which she had shown the hurt was to keep pretty much to herself after the marriage, and to see as little as possible of Johann and Henrietta.

Surely, thought Johann now, surely he might have done *something* toward making his mother happier. If he had been less busy—? Or, perhaps, more unselfish—? Actually, there was little he could have done. He had remained Mother Strauss's loving and considerate child, even after his marriage; but Henrietta had become "his destiny."

Before he could recover from this shock, another blow fell. On July 21, 1870—only five months later—his brother Josef followed their mother. At his death Josef was only forty-three. Always high-strung and sensitive, he had lately been subjected to several unhappy experiences that combined to aggravate his nervous illness and finally to kill him.

For the past few seasons Josef had been substituting for Johann at the Pavlovsk concerts. Then, when the directors of the resort decided—after twelve seasons altogether—not to renew the Strauss contract, Josef persuaded himself that it was his fault. If, he said bitterly, Johann had been doing the conducting, surely the orchestra would have been re-engaged; obviously the Russians had no use for a second-rate substitute! Johann, of course, tried to convince him that it was not his fault at all—that probably, even if Johann *had* been doing the conducting, the contract wouldn't have been renewed; perhaps the directors just wanted to make a change in the type of music offered at Pavlovsk, after all these years. . . . But it was in vain; Josef went on brooding.

On Mother Strauss's death, the brooding turned into melancholia. In his life she had always been the most important element, and as long as she lived she had been able to cheer him up, or at least to console him when things went wrong. Without her, he felt lost. His headaches, fainting spells, and other nervous disorders were now continuous. He knew—and frequently said—that he had not much longer to live.

During the early summer of 1870 Josef was conducting a concert in Warsaw when one of the violinists, disregarding directions, failed to take a certain repeat in a waltz. Since all the other players did take the repeat, and only that one man went on to play the new section, the resulting chaos may be imagined! But it was really a minor matter, the kind of accident that occasionally happens to the best of café-house conductors. By now, however, it took little to make Josef's taut nerves snap, and he collapsed on the stage and had to be carried off. Brought back to Vienna, he was found to have a lesion of the brain. From this he never recovered; and on July 21 he died.

Josef's death brings us to an episode involving "Edi" —the youngest Strauss brother, and the least lovable. Eduard was what would today be called an opportunist, prone to take the shortest and easiest way to securing his own interests; and he was now facing a difficult decision.

Two years before, Josef had begged Eduard to enter into a solemn pact with him: Whichever of the two survived was to destroy all the other's manuscript music. Josef's reason for wanting all his unpublished works forgotten was that he had never believed that the music he had written for café-house concerts did justice to his real gifts. A few of his pieces had been printed and published; these, of course, could not now be taken out of circulation. But whatever was still in manuscript at the time of his death, he wanted destroyed. And he would do the same by Edi in case the latter died first. Would Edi agree?

Edi, however, was easy-going, and his musical standards were not so high as Josef's. Indeed, he was rather proud of the pieces he had written. So he demurred at first. What did he care, he asked gaily, what people thought of him and his music after his death? "They can put it into a museum, or paper the walls of the café-houses with it if they like!" But his levity was dissipated a moment later by the look in Josef's eyes— those severe, unhappy eyes, already resigned to the prospect of death not too far in the future. So Eduard, on his side, made the promise.

And now Josef was dead, and Eduard was finding it hard to carry out the thing that Josef had trusted him to do. Looking through the manuscripts Josef had left —a fairly large collection of arrangements, potpourris, and original compositions—he found so much that was characteristically beautiful that destroying it would be like destroying a part of the Josef he had loved so dearly. So Eduard temporized. "Not just now; no need to decide in a hurry; some day I'll get around to doing it." It was something like this that he told himself as he looked at the manuscripts.

And so the years passed, with Eduard continuing to

play Josef's music, and continuing to put off the fulfillment of his promise. For thirty-seven years his conscience struggled with his love of Josef's music. At last, in 1907 —when his own career was over!—he decided in favor of his oath; he took the huge load of music manuscript to a furnace near by, and burned it sheet by sheet. Perhaps it is hard to blame him for his reluctance, since this act wiped out nearly everything that Josef had written. Still, a promise is a promise. . . .

Now, all that remained of Josef's work were the few pieces he had published in his lifetime. But these pieces —particularly *Dorfschwalben, Delirienwalzer, Sphärenklänge,* and *Aquarellenwalzer*—prove his right to belong permanently to the magistral line of great waltz composers.

CHAPTER XX

A New World to Conquer

WHEN, IN 1864, Jacques Offenbach visited Vienna for
the Carnival season, it was inevitable that he should
meet Johann Strauss. He admired the younger man immensely, and as the two musicians sat in the Goldenes
Lamm café sipping wine, they exchanged pleasantries
and compliments. The genius of the opéra-comique—
the thin, lanky Frenchman with quick blue eyes behind

a pince-nez, and a dagger-point wit; and the genius of the waltz—the suave Viennese, his rich crop of hair and spreading mustache still untouched by gray, his sensitive fingers nervously alive every moment as though they were playing some invisible violin—between them these two dominated the light music of Europe!

Three years later, as we have already seen in a previous chapter, Strauss was to receive a hero's acclaim in Paris. Now, in 1864, Vienna first paid tribute to Offenbach. No fewer than three of his operettas were playing simultaneously in three different theaters. Vienna loved these operettas, especially that masterpiece *Orpheus in the Underworld,* because it saw in them a finer and wittier type of farce than the kind it was accustomed to on its own stage. The styles of Offenbach and Strauss had different shades and hues: Strauss had the sentimentality and tenderness of the Viennese; Offenbach, the sharp wit and mocking irony of the Parisian. But they spoke a universal tongue, though in different accents—a language of gaiety and beauty which made each one of them welcome outside of his own immediate precincts.

While they were talking at the Goldenes Lamm, Offenbach asked Strauss: "Why don't *you* write an operetta—you, with your natural genius?"

It was the first time that the idea had occurred to Strauss of extending his horizon beyond the constricted periphery of the café-house waltz.

Strauss smiled at the flattery. "Invade *your* territory,

my friend? Why, I should only meet defeat in the face of such a strong opponent! No, thank you!"

"Generous words, Herr Strauss, and probably sincere, too. But with your originality and imagination you need not be afraid of invading any man's territory. It is we who should be afraid of you!"

Strauss drummed his fingertips on the table as he considered this new idea. "No," he said finally. "I'm a waltz composer. And it is a long step from the café-house to the theater."

Offenbach adjusted his pince-nez. "Well, far be it from me to persuade you! You would only prove a dangerous rival!" And the subject was dropped.

But the idea that Offenbach had planted in Strauss's mind refused to be forgotten. Again and again he reflected on it, and presently it began to attract him. He was aware that in the writing of waltzes he had reached the zenith of his creative powers; further in this form he could not go. Undoubtedly he would compose many more waltzes, and they would be good ones—but in doing this he would be standing still, repeating himself. The theater, however—that was something else! The theater would spread before him a far greater canvas than he had ever had, would offer an absolutely new medium for him, a more ambitious medium.

When he repeated to Henrietta what Offenbach had suggested, she was at once all enthusiasm. Having once been a prima donna she had the blood of the theater in her veins. Now, if she could no longer bask in the lime-lights herself, she could enjoy them through her Johann.

"Why, to be sure, Schani!" she cried. "Why didn't *I* think of that? Operetta is exactly the medium for you. Offenbach is right. Why shouldn't the Waltz King become the King of Operetta as well?"

But Johann was still reluctant. "How do I know that I should be successful?" he demanded. "It would be a big risk for a man in my position, Jetty. You know the Viennese—you know just how they regard me. But let me take one false step, lay myself open to ridicule with one real failure—and it will be Good-by, Herr Strauss! 'Poor Strauss,' they will say; 'he is written out.' And they will turn to somebody new."

For all his doubts, though, he himself had already been considering the idea even while he discussed it with Henrietta. Indeed, he had started some sketches for an operetta. Now, impatiently and brusquely, he pushed these aside. No—the game wasn't worth the candle, the cobbler should stick to his last, and so forth! Let Offenbach write the operettas; *he* would keep on writing waltzes. And so he did, for a few years more.

But he had been reckoning without Henrietta—her strong will, her ambition for him, her resourcefulness. It was in the fall of 1870 that she decided she had waited long enough for Johann to write his operetta. She would now take matters into her own hands. She went to Johann's friend, Maximilian Steiner, director of the Theater-an-der-Wien, and asked him how he would like to put on a Strauss operetta. She did not have to wait for an answer; Steiner's eyes sparkled at the prospect!

"Very well," she said; "but you will have to help me. If we play our hand well, we'll win."

And she explained the plan. She took out a bundle of manuscripts—Strauss's spasmodic and abandoned attempts at operetta writing. "Have one of your poets write words to some of these tunes," she suggested. "Then let's stage it for Johann. When he sees for himself how well the pieces sound, I'm sure he'll be won over completely."

And so, one afternoon, Henrietta invited Johann to the Theater-an-der-Wien to hear "a rehearsal of some operetta scenes by a promising young composer." "Max thinks highly of the young musician," she added, "and he wants your opinion. I promised him that you would come."

In the dark theater the audience consisted of three persons: Steiner, Strauss, and Henrietta. The curtain rose. The orchestra struck up the opening bars. Strauss, startled, twisted uneasily in his seat and began to breathe faster. Then—after a few more bars—the point dawned on him. The scene gradually unfolded, and he laughed aloud. "I seem," he whispered to Henrietta, "to detect *your* delicate hand in these proceedings!"

The experiment proved highly successful. Here, for Strauss, was incontrovertible evidence that his music *could* sound well in the theater—which in turn convinced him that, if he applied himself to it, he could write a good operetta. Yes, he was now ready to give his word to Steiner: he would write an operetta for the Theater-an-der-Wien. Immediately.

Operetta, comic-opera, opéra-comique, opera buffa—they are all branches of the same tree. And the roots of this tree reach back to the early 18th century when an Italian composer named Pergolesi wrote the first comic opera in musical history, *La Serva padrona.*

Before Pergolesi's time, comic characters in comic scenes (called Intermezzi) were often interpolated in Italian opera, and were extremely popular with the audiences. But Pergolesi's *La Serva padrona,* composed in 1733, was the first complete comic opera. It was a simple story calling for only three characters, with no chorus or ballet. Set to crisp, engaging, sprightly music, it is a work of exquisite perfection, sparkling with phosphorescent wit.

La Serva padrona made musical history. Twenty years after its première in Naples, it was introduced elsewhere in Europe by itinerant companies, and wherever it went it was received enthusiastically.

In France, this opera was instrumental in creating a new art form. First, the French composers Monsigny and Grétry were inspired by the Pergolesi work to write comic operas that became models for their successors in France. After them came that great triumvirate of opéra-comique: Boïeldieu (composer of *La Dame blanche*), Auber (*Fra Diavolo*), and Adam (*Le Postillon de Longjumeau*). With the work of these three men, the form of the French opéra-comique was set and integrated. And from them it is but a short step to the brilliant masterpieces of Jacques Offenbach—who was born in

Germany in 1819 but who early went to Paris and made it his permanent home.

In Italy, the influence of *La Serva padrona* resulted in the emergence of "opera buffa" through the works of such early masters as Paisiello and Piccinni. From these composers we pass directly to that greatest of all masters of Italian opera buffa, Rossini.

In Germany, too, the influence of *La Serva padrona* was felt. It has been said that the Pergolesi opera furnished the inspiration for the German *Singspiel*—a comedy interspersed with popular songs and ensemble pieces, and the direct predecessor of the German operetta. The creator of the *Singspiel* was Johann Adam Hiller; out of his works developed the comic operas of Mozart and the early operettas of Albert Lortzing. Traveling in a straight line from Lortzing, we arrive at the operettas of Franz von Suppé and Johann Strauss.

But the Strauss operetta was formed also by still another major influence: the Viennese satirical play developed by such native sons as the poet Ferdinand Raimund and the dramatist Johann Nestroy. This type of dramatic satire, born among the people, was presented in the Vienna market-places by itinerant actors.

Thus, when Johann Strauss began writing his operettas, they were something like a great river into which flow many smaller streams. Strauss's musical deftness, the nimble rhythms, the fleet staccato figures, the often beautifully sculptured melodic line—all these were derived from Pergolesi, the later Italian opera buffa, and the *Singspiel*. The sophistication, the finesse, the delicate irony, came from the French opéra-comique. And to the Viennese popular theater Strauss was indebted for his acidulous satire and his occasional recourse to either parody or symbolism.

To all these elements Strauss was to add a fresh one original with him: his infectious dances, his polkas, quadrilles, and incomparable waltzes.

His mind now made up, Johann Strauss started his first operetta. He shut himself in his study, writing page after page of music, smoking incessantly, often working through half the night. Occasionally he took a short nap, or relaxed over a game of billiards with a friend. But always he was restless to get back to his task.

His first attempt was a satire on the founding of Rome, called *Romulus;* but he soon discarded this. Then he turned to a gay and light book called *The Merry Wives of Vienna,* and actually finished the entire score. But it was destined never to be produced. The star for whom the operetta was written, and without whom it could not be produced, quarreled with Steiner and broke her contract with the theater. The work was then shelved permanently.

Strauss's third project—the operetta that was eventually produced—was *Indigo and the Forty Thieves.* Built on a rather silly libretto which was the work of many collaborators, the operetta was so confused in plot that one despairs of resolving it into an intelligible pattern. Strauss, however, was not discouraged by this fact, and his pen flew in his hand.

Vienna was truly excited when it learned that its favorite composer, its own Schani, had written an operetta; that *Indigo* was to be produced on February 10, 1871, on the historic stage of the Theater-an-der-Wien which had introduced such masterpieces as Beethoven's *Fidelio* and Mozart's *Die Zauberflöte*. Long before the evening of the première the house was sold out. The première itself was one of the most important theatrical events of several years, attended by everybody who was anybody in Vienna.

On his way to the theater to conduct the opening performance, Johann felt faint with nervousness. *Indigo and the Forty Thieves* suddenly seemed to him a shabby work, a fraud, which would at one stroke demolish all that he had built up so carefully in twenty-five years. But once in the theater, he discovered that his usual self-assurance was back. "Just as of old in the dance halls he swung himself boldly up to his desk," reported Speidel. "One flaming glance darted to the right, a second flaming glance to the left, and then the signal to begin. And when the brilliant principal number of the evening resounded, the waltz *Ja, so singt man in der Stadt wo ich geboren bin,* the whole house broke out into cries of jubilation, the occupants of the boxes and orchestra stalls began to sway in dance time. Then it seemed as if Strauss must snatch the nearest player's violin, draw his bow across it and—as he had been wont to do at the Sperl, at the Zeisig, and at Dommayer's—begin to play for the people to dance."

The evening, in short, was a phenomenal triumph

for Strauss. They cheered him in the theater, and sang his praises in the press. Who cared or knew what the title meant, or what the text contained, so long as there were polkas, quadrilles, and waltzes, all written in Strauss's most engaging vein? Ah, said the Viennese, there was no one like Schani for writing melodies that were as heart-warming as new wine. *"Ja, so singt man, ja, so singt man in der Stadt wo ich geboren bin!"* (Yes, so one sings, so one sings in the city of my birth!) and *"Dort an der blauen Donau möcht ich gehen"* (There by the blue Danube, there I'd like to go)—these were words the audience understood, words about a city filled with song, hard by "the beautiful blue Danube," and expressed in typically Straussian song!

e.c.

CHAPTER XXI

When America Was Musically Young

IN 1872 THE CITY of Boston launched a monster Jubilee
to commemorate the centenary of the proposal of the
State of Massachusetts to separate itself from England.
This celebration was to include a prodigious music festival, planned and directed by the famous American bandleader, Patrick S. Gilmore. For this occasion, Johann
Strauss, now a world figure, was invited to direct his
own works. Strauss was not eager to go. He had always
detested travel, and was even a little afraid of crossing
the ocean. But he was tempted by the $100,000 fee—
the highest that America had thus far offered a foreign
musician. And Henrietta, ever hungry for new triumphs
for her husband, was insistent on going. On June 1,

1872, therefore, the Strausses left for the New World, and on June 15 they arrived in New York.

Both before and after the Strauss visit here, we in America were very backward in our musical culture, America's phenomenal advance in music being essentially a 20th-century development. In those days we were musically young, awkward, ingenuous. European musicians who toured this country used to brighten their conversations at home with amusing anecdotes illustrating our musical innocence.

What appealed to Americans then was the sensational, the bizarre, the gigantic. It was the era during which P. T. Barnum rose to popularity. Indeed, it was Barnum who in 1850 took the great Jenny Lind under his managerial wing when she made her first tour of this country. This was as it should have been at the time, for it was through circus devices that music appealed to the larger American public: exploiting eccentric personalities, introducing breath-taking extra-musical novelties, featuring unexpected tricks.

Besides the sensational, American audiences fell also for the grandiose. The bigger the attraction, the more warmly it was appreciated. Recitals by a single artist were virtually unknown until Anton Rubinstein essayed one in New York in 1873. To make an impression, a concert needed an array of artists—the more the merrier—plus a large orchestra and a huge chorus. We liked sixteen people playing on eight pianos, orchestras numbering hundreds of members, massed choruses rising impressively until the heads of the rear rows of singers almost touched the scenery above. A performance of the "Anvil Chorus" from *Il Trovatore* at Chickering Hall, New York, enlisted the services of one hundred firemen who banged out the rhythms of the chorus on real anvils!

That American audiences in those days had musical tastes and standards that were immature, if not actually childish, is proved when we look at the kind of music played at the concerts. Not for them an uninterrupted evening of "heavy" music! Straight symphonic programs gradually came to be tolerated and then welcomed in the larger and more sophisticated centers; but in the smaller places orchestral concerts usually had to program dance music between symphony movements, and chamber-music groups must include light "salon pieces" and transcriptions of popular favorites if they wanted people to listen to Haydn and Mozart.

Such, in general, was the state of musical taste in America when Strauss arrived, and it was a framework into which he fitted gracefully.

When he reached Boston, on June 17, 1872, he was given a regal reception. The streets, lined with crowds, rang with wild enthusiasm. Women struggled through the mob to touch his cape, or to kiss its hem; some even tried to clip off locks of his hair! Men begged for his autograph. Throughout the city, huge placards were displayed picturing Strauss as the musical monarch of the world: he was shown sitting on top of the globe, violin and bow in hand.

A special Coliseum capable of accommodating a hundred thousand spectators (with a stage large enough for several thousand musicians!) was built for the Festival in the Back Bay section of the city. Here Strauss was scheduled to participate in fourteen concerts. At his American debut, on June 17 (the inaugural concert of the festival), the place was packed to the doors and the roof. Six policemen had to plow a path for Strauss through the dense crowds collected outside the hall.

It was a concert cut to American specifications. It offered a strange mélange of musical oddities. Operatic excerpts and orchestral numbers by Wagner, Mendelssohn, Rossini, Verdi, and Donizetti were heard together with patriotic songs and hymns. Mammoth ensembles played these numbers, and in some of the patriotic pieces the Gargantuan musical forces were supplemented by cannon and anvils. Strauss himself conducted only one number, *The Blue Danube*—the fifth feature on the program. Strauss has left us a vivid description of that performance:

"On the musicians' tribune there were twenty thousand singers; in front of them, the members of the orchestra—and these were the people I was to conduct. A hundred assistant conductors had been placed at my disposal to control these gigantic masses, but I was able only to recognize those nearest to me; and although we had rehearsals there was no possibility of giving an artistic performance, a proper production. . . .

"Now just conceive of my position, face to face with a public of four hundred thousand Americans. There I stood at the raised desk, high above all the others. How would the business start? How would it end? Suddenly a cannon shot rang out, a gentle hint for us twenty thousand to begin playing *The Blue Danube.*

"I gave the signal, my hundred assistant conductors followed me as quickly and as well as they could—and then there broke out an unholy row such as I shall never forget. As we had begun more or less simultaneously, I concentrated my whole attention on seeing that we should finish together, too! Thank Heaven, I managed even that. It was all that was humanly possible. The hundred thousand mouths in the audience roared approbation and I breathed a sigh of relief when I found myself in fresh air again and felt the firm ground underneath my feet."

In these fourteen concerts, Strauss played some of his most famous pieces, one at every concert. On June 18, *Wine, Woman, and Song;* on June 20, *A Thousand and One Nights;* on June 21, *Morgenblätter;* on June 22, *New Vienna (Neu-Wien) Waltz.* He even wrote some new pieces for this gala occasion. One of these, called *Walzerbouquet,* was a potpourri of his most famous waltzes. Another was the *New Jubilee Waltz,* which closed with *The Star-Spangled Banner* played in three-quarter time!

Each one of his appearances vied with the others in hysterical demonstration. The newspapers exhausted their vocabulary of laudatory adjectives in describing his magic, his personality, his art. "We must object to Herr Strauss driving Boston waltz-mad," one paper said. The music critic of another, surveying the festival as a whole, wrote: "The chief honors, from a strictly musical point of view, were, in our judgment, carried off by Herr Strauss." And *The Weekly Review* confessed editorially: "We have learned something from Herr Johann Strauss. Let us admit that we were wrong and that he has set us right. It has been our practice to play waltzes too fast. . . . Hear a waltz played by Thomas's orchestra and the same by Strauss's band, and you hardly recognize it as the identical piece. Not only does the former take the tempo too quick, but he fails consequently to give it that variety of expression without which the performance is mere mechanism. It is really wonderful how a *pianissimo* or a *forte,* a *ritardando* or a *crescendo,* an emphatic accent or other mark of expression animates, improves, and heightens the effect of a piece. It gives it life and color at once, and all this has been observed and will never be forgotten by all who heard Strauss's waltzes performed under Strauss's direction."

He was begged to tour the entire country; offers deluged him. But Johann was homesick for Vienna. All these lavish demonstrations were sapping his energy, exhausting him physically. He wanted to go home. But he was prevailed upon to give four additional concerts in New York, at the Academy of Music, home of grand opera. At these he was only one of several attractions; other orchestral numbers were directed by Carl Bergmann, the principal conductor of the New York Philharmonic Orchestra, and there were also operatic and instrumental soloists. But New York had eyes and ears only for Strauss. At the first concert he played *Artists' Life, The Blue Danube, Pizzicato Polka, Tritsch-Tratsch Polka;* at the second, *Morgenblätter, A Thousand and One Nights, Tritsch-Tratsch Polka.* And so it went. The audiences simply could not get enough of Strauss and his music. "Would that he remained with us permanently!" exclaimed one New York journalist regretfully.

But not all the triumphs in the world could make Strauss forget that his place was in Vienna. Refusing all further offers, he left America in mid-July, and two weeks afterward was at home again.

CHAPTER XXII

A Hymn to Champagne

IN THE PRATER DISTRICT of Vienna were spread the magnificent buildings and exhibits of the International Fair of 1873. Two years in the planning and developed on Gargantuan lines, the exhibition was expected to dwarf all other affairs of the kind ever before held elsewhere. In its honor, Vienna was in gala mood, and all the overpowering adjectives favored by the period were utilized to describe the program in prospect: grand balls, splendid dinner parties, stupendous state ceremonials, monumental entertainments.

When the exhibition opened in May, it attracted what was perhaps the most imposing assemblage of European notables ever to have gathered in one city at one time; certainly Vienna itself had not played host to so distinguished a galaxy since the Congress of Vienna some sixty years before.

But the evil fate pursuing Emperor Francis Joseph was still at his heels, and once more his country was to suffer. Just a week after the opening of the exhibition, catastrophe struck Vienna: a disastrous bank failure brought on a financial crisis that swept away fortunes, sent many a great establishment down to ruin, swelled the ranks of the unemployed, and started an epidemic of suicides. Nor was Austria the only country to enter a period of depression. The year 1873 was a bad one for all Europe, and in the autumn there began in the United States one of the worst panics in our history.

Johann Strauss, who was of course a leading attraction at the Vienna Fair (as was also his brother Eduard), at once composed a waltz in order to buoy up the depressed spirits of his fellow-Viennese, and it was to become one of his most celebrated. *Wiener Blut* was a bravely ringing affirmation that *"das Weahner geht nicht unter"*—or, in our modern phrase, the Viennese may be down, but he's never out!

As if to give further point to so cheering an assurance, Strauss followed *Wiener Blut* with the gayest, most effervescent masterpiece to leave his pen—the operetta *Die Fledermaus.*

Steiner of the Theater-an-der-Wien had provided Strauss with a gay little play called *Reveillon,* the work of two Frenchmen, Meilhac and Halévy, who had provided Offenbach with many of his librettos. This play had been adapted for Viennese audiences by Haffner and Genée. Now called *Die Fledermaus,* it reached Strauss's hands as possible material for a new operetta. Strauss, who always liked animals, was immediately attracted to the title, *The Bat.* But the play especially caught his fancy. It concerned the escapade of one Eisenstein who, supposed to report to prison to serve a brief term for a slight offense, proceeds instead to a masquerade given at the palace of Prince Orloff. To the same ball comes Eisenstein's wife, Rosalinda, unaware of the fact that her husband is there. A gay flirtation develops between husband and wife, neither of whom—since both are masked and disguised—gathers the other's identity.

Once more shutting himself in his study—his privacy jealously guarded by Henrietta—Strauss spent forty-two days of hard work on his score. During this period he was a stranger to the outside world. His food was brought to him on a tray to be eaten at such moments as he could snatch from his work. Not a friend saw him, except Steiner and Genée who came to discuss details with him.

At last, there it was—the final draft of *Die Fledermaus.* Looking over the pages of the manuscript, Strauss had good reason for satisfaction. His music, catching magically the insouciant, gay, and piquant tone of the play, was ironic and saucy. And at the scene of the Prince's masquerade ball, he had succeeded in creating one of his most striking and picturesque passages, culminating in a waltz which—with its opening sharp eighth-notes—makes the blood tingle:

A toast to His Majesty—
Long live Champagne the First!

—a paean of praise to the prince of wines that set the atmosphere and tempo of the whole operetta. Truly, *Die Fledermaus* was as frothy, as bubbling with zest, as intoxicating as the champagne which it hymned!

A brilliant audience attended the première of *Die Fledermaus,* at the Theater-an-der-Wien on April 5, 1874. It acclaimed Strauss's new operetta boisterously. But the critics, headed by Eduard Hanslick, did not like it. Some of them felt that it was bad taste on the part of Strauss to write a glorification of King Champagne at a time when the Viennese still suffered from the after-effects of a major economic collapse. Some of them said, besides—and somewhat contemptuously—that Strauss had brought the café-house into the theater. Little did they suspect that in such criticism they were actually expressing the highest praise. For the music of *Die Fledermaus* had none of the affectations and false attitudes which one might reasonably expect in a work of a café-house musician composing a serious and ambitious work. In it, Johann Strauss remained himself. The music of *Die Fledermaus* has all the grace and movement and poise of his best waltzes, all the subtle nuances, all the exquisite sensitivity. The humor is deft, sparkling with ironic glitter. The supply of rich and intoxicating melodies seems inexhaustible. And some of them—like the

Hymn to Champagne, and the *Du und Du* waltz—remain the most eloquent productions that Strauss has left us, the work of a popular composer who was a genius.

It was the critics who decided the immediate fate of *Die Fledermaus:* after sixteen performances it was withdrawn from the repertory—apparently a failure. Eventually, however, it was the audiences who decided its real destiny. But they decided that destiny not in Vienna but —as earlier in the case of *The Blue Danube*—elsewhere in Europe. Introduced in Berlin soon after the Vienna première, the work was a sensation. The audiences packed the theater, sang *Fledermaus* melodies, and heartily loved its charm and wit. Steiner, noting the Berliners' response, resolved to give the work a second chance in Vienna. Reintroduced to it, the Viennese public (which had liked it originally) demonstrated its approval even more strongly than before—and the audience swept the critics with it on the tide of its acclaim.

Then began the march of *Die Fledermaus* around the world. In Hamburg it had two hundred performances. In Paris, it was added successfully (in a somewhat garbled version) to the repertory of the Renaissance Theater. In New York, it was heard at the Germania Theater only eight months after the original Vienna première! And its popularity continued to grow and grow. Fine productions were given in most of the European capitals, including one at the Théâtre des Variétés in Paris. In 1905 it was put on magnificently at the Metropolitan Opera House in New York.

And it has since become the most famous and best-loved of all operettas. Time does not seem to stale its youthful charm and grace. Again and again it is revived; and—withstanding all changes in customs and idioms and manners—again and again it triumphs anew. As recently as 1943 it was restored to the Broadway theater under the title *Rosalinda,* and characteristically became one of the leading hits of the season.

It has long been customary in many of the great European opera houses to perform *Die Fledermaus* as part of the regular repertory, and with the dignity and painstaking artistic care generally given only to serious opera. This is as great a tribute as any—greater, perhaps, than that represented by its popularity—to the originality and importance of Strauss's music. He wrote his operetta for the delectation and entertainment of the masses; but because he was an inspired composer, a rather slight and trivial plot and a gay popular-music idiom were transformed by his Midas touch into the gold of a work of art.

CHAPTER XXIII

Grand Seigneur of the Igelgasse

IN 1874 VIENNA CEREMONIOUSLY CELEBRATED the thirtieth anniversary of the founding of the Strauss band. It was honoring one who not only was its most famous composer of the period, but who also had by now become something of a *grand seigneur*. Strauss had bought a villa at Ischl, the luxurious resort near Vienna, and in the city proper he had built for himself and Henrietta a palace on the Igelgasse. In either place, he could now

143

stroll about his "estate" wearing a handsome silk dressing-gown and smoking a cigarette—and reflecting on how agreeable the world was!

"He is tall, good-looking, with a black mustache and flowing black whiskers," was one newspaper's description at this time. "His black hair, brushed back, reveals a fine, imposing forehead. A quick expressive eye and a genial expression give his face a pleasant air. He is always elegantly dressed in the latest fashion. And he is a ladies' man."

Strauss had few diversions. Books were not among his pleasures; when he read anything it was usually a newspaper or a magazine. Though he liked people immensely, he did not enjoy social functions of any sort. Though this is hard to believe, he was never much of a dancer, and therefore avoided balls and public dances. He much preferred an intimate tête-à-tête with one or two personal friends at his own home. He no longer spent much time in the café-house. His leisure hours were usually passed over a game of billiards or cards, either in the company of friends or with Henrietta.

When people wanted to see him, they visited him at his home: men like Johann Herbeck, famous conductor and one of the most influential musicians in Vienna; or like the pianists Anton Rubinstein, Franz Liszt, and Grünfeld, all of whom had played Strauss waltzes on their recital programs. As a host he was cordial, diffusing genial warmth among his guests; and every gathering at the Igelgasse was enlivened by his fine sense of humor and his gift for a wittily turned phrase.

One of his intimate friends and ardent admirers was Johannes Brahms. In 1874 Brahms, at forty-one, was already a musician of some consequence in Vienna. He conducted the celebrated Singakademie, and his choral and chamber music had been heard and admired. (His First Symphony was not to be heard in Vienna until two years later, on December 17, 1876.) A strange friendship this! The two men were of different musical worlds—the popular and the serious; yet they were linked each by admiration for the other's genius, each by a tolerant recognition of the other's right to his artistic convictions.

But Brahms and Johann Strauss were opposites outside of art as well as inside. Brahms (already wearing his patriarchal beard) was short, squat, brusque in his behavior, frequently ill-mannered, his words (uttered in falsetto) often barbed and cutting. Strauss was tall, handsome, the essence of courtly manners, always gentle, considerate, affectionate, incapable of a cruel word. Yet the two men were drawn to each other, and took genuine pleasure in each other's company. And how sincerely Brahms did admire Strauss! There was never the least touch of condescension in his attitude towards his fellow-musician, but rather a healthy respect, and even a suggestion of envy! He never tired of praising Strauss's gift of melody, his endless charm and freshness. One of the last musical events that Brahms attended toward the close of his life was the première of Strauss's final operetta, *Die Göttin der Vernunft;* this was on March 13, 1897, three weeks before Brahms's death. Though in the clutch of his final illness and suffering acute pain, he stayed in the theater until the end of the performance, unable to tear himself away from the Strauss music!

Strauss's travels were now few and far between: he liked nothing better than to stay at home with Henrietta and absorb the peace and luxury of familiar surroundings. But on those rare occasions when he did leave Austria it was only to rediscover how firmly rooted his fame was everywhere. In the spring of 1874, he took his orchestra for a tour of Italy. His triumph there was so splendid that it was said that single-handed he had accomplished more than had any diplomat in effecting a more cordial relation between Austria and Italy, so lately at war with each other.

His one and only passion was—work. Composing absorbed him so completely that he had little time or inclination for anything else. He wrote waltzes and operettas tirelessly. He was always scribbling notes. Even in the company of friends, or in the midst of a game of cards, he would furtively reach for the nearest available paper so as to jot down a few ideas. He wrote on the first thing that came to his hand: a menu, a napkin, a handkerchief, his linen cuffs. Sometimes, when in bed, he would be struck by a brilliant thought or melody and would there and then note it down on the bedsheet. He seemed always to be bursting with melodies, and never to lose his innate joy in writing music. . . .

CHAPTER XXIV

"You Are My Peace"

IN 1878 HENRIETTA DIED of a heart attack, and died alone. Johann returned from the café-house to find her lying on the floor lifeless.

As it had been when his mother died, Strauss could not bear the thought of someone so near and dear to him being buried, so he left the funeral arrangements to his brother Eduard and himself fled to Italy. When he came back to Vienna, he was a changed man: morose, self-contained, restless, lonely. He refused to return to his palace on the Igelgasse, which suddenly seemed ghostly bare to him. Instead he made his home in one of Vienna's fine hotels, the Victoria. His life, up to now so orderly and of an even course, became overnight confused and chaotic. He was at a loss to systematize his daily routine.

Nor was his loneliness to be overcome by the society of friends, of whom he had never known any lack. What he needed was another Henrietta—to be with him all the time, to watch over his intricate affairs, to serve as friend and counselor in one, to create for him an atmosphere of serenity and peace. In short, he was ripe for another marriage.

One day, a young and strikingly beautiful voice-student named Angelika Diettrich called to ask him to give her lessons. Actually it was not singing that interested her, but Strauss. She had for some time worshipped the Waltz King from a distance. At last, hearing that Strauss's wife had died, she decided to win him for herself. And one had merely to glance at her firm lips, and at the direct and forceful expression of her eyes, to realize that what Angelika went after, she usually got!

Johann, lonely and unhappy, responded as might have been expected to a young girl's softness, tenderness, admiration. Inevitably, her charm and her youth (she was only twenty) attracted him. Besides, she was so solicitous about his well-being, so effusive in her affection, so coy and winsome! Johann, who the past few months had known only winter, felt suddenly as if spring had returned. He decided that he was in love; and, yearning for the orderliness of a happy domestic life, he saw in Angelika the answer to his need. He swept aside the fact that she was so much younger—thirty years, no less. He remained deaf to the warnings of his friends, who knew how impossible Angelika was. And when he asked her to marry him, she consented—not because she loved Johann, but because she wanted to be the wife of a rich and famous man. She played her game skillfully, and she won. Strauss, bringing her into his beautiful home in the Igelgasse, trusted that she would at least partly fill the void left by Henrietta's death.

It was an unhappy marriage from the first. Angelika —Lily, for short—did not love Johann; she never had loved him. And Johann soon realized that he had mistaken his own feelings. Besides, the two were worlds apart. Apart in age: Johann, now in his middle years, wanted nothing so much as quiet, peace, stability; Lily was young, light-headed, full of restlessness and unsatisfied yearnings. Marriage promptly taught her that there was not much glamour in a man who preferred to sit in his study all the time writing music, while she craved pleasure, gaiety, champagne, café-houses, balls. And they were apart in spirit: Lily was totally uncultivated, stupid about art and music, incapable of appreciating her husband's genius. His sedateness irritated her; his talk about his music, his aims, his aspirations, bored her to tears. She now saw Strauss in a new light—as a sad, tired, old man—and she could hardly stand him!

The five years of this marriage were among the unhappiest of Johann's life. Towards the end of this period they led separate lives, little concerned with each other's activities. Finally, they were divorced.

Johann married for a third time soon after his divorce from Lily. And now he found the rest for which he had been longing, for his third wife was of Henrietta's fiber. Her name was Adele Deutsch, and Johann had known her, and liked her, since she was a child. She was attractive, with intense dark eyes and Jewish features. She was warm-hearted and considerate, and she worshipped Johann. During her marriage (to a man named Deutsch) Johann often visited her; and through all the terrible years with Lily, Adele's sympathy and advice were a tonic that helped his spirits. Then Herr Deutsch died; Johann was divorced; and the two were drawn together even more closely. In Adele's home, which he now visited daily, he found the peace he hungered for. He would sit there in slippers and dressing-gown, telling Adele about his past and his hopes for the future. And he knew, as he spoke, that here was someone who knew him and understood him.

It seemed natural that they should get married, for they had now become inseparable, had reached such mutual dependence that each felt it impossible to go on living without the other.

Adele brought into the Igelgasse house a warmth and a glow it had not known for years. With her, Johann was able to thaw, at last to be himself again. As in the case of his first marriage, domestic happiness inspired him anew. He had not been idle during his years with Lily; but the music he wrote at this time was too often stilted and without heart. Now, with Adele to encourage him, music once again coursed from him in an uninterrupted flow. Because of Henrietta he had written his first great waltzes and *Die Fledermaus*. Now, because of Adele, he could write other magnificent waltzes, like the *Frühlingsstimmen* ("Voices of Spring" because spring had come back to him!), and the operetta *Der Zigeunerbaron* which was to come in his sixtieth year, 1884.

CHAPTER XXV

King Johann the Second

A PARALLEL might be drawn between any of Strauss's waltzes and the course of his life. The waltz has an Introduction, in which the themes to come are glimpsed and foreshadowed. So with Strauss's life: think of his boyhood struggles to express himself in music, particularly in waltzes. Next in the waltz itself comes the chain of varying melodies—and his life had its happy passages and its sad ones, alternating and intermingling. And the waltz ends with a coda, which casts a reminiscent glance back at the main themes of the composition. Strauss's life, too, finished with a coda that summarized his achievements. Actually there were two codas, the second one coming ten years after the first.

As the first coda we may take the year 1884, in which Strauss celebrated the fortieth anniversary of his career as café-house Kapellmeister. Never before had Vienna rendered such honor to a musician. The streets were decorated with banners and flags. Officials in every walk of life, from the Emperor down, paid him tribute. There was hardly an organization, musical or other, that did not offer him some token of recognition. Medals and diplomas were sent him from near and far. Cordial letters and telegrams of praise came from his many friends throughout the world. There were gifts in an unending procession: from musicians such as Verdi and Brahms; from Bismarck and other statesmen; from Suppé and Millöcker and many another rival operetta composer.

The week of celebration culminated in a monumental concert at the Theater-an-der-Wien. It was then and there that the first coda of Strauss's life-waltz was heard. Scenes from his best-known operettas were performed, and all his great waltzes. The applause grew and mounted until, after *The Blue Danube,* it sounded like a peal of thunder. At last, Strauss himself came to the stage. The audience rose to its feet and acclaimed him with a swelling chorus that was deafening.

"I am deeply touched," Strauss said simply; "so deeply that it is hard for me to put my feelings into words. I can only say this now—and you know that it comes from the bottom of my heart: Thank you. Thank you very much, beloved citizens of Vienna!"

A few minutes later the Emperor himself paid personal homage to Strauss. "Strauss," he said, pointing to the wildly enthusiastic audience, "you *too* are Emperor!"

As if in further expression of his gratitude to Vienna for such an overwhelming demonstration of love and admiration, Johann Strauss soon afterwards presented the city and its citizens with one of the last of his great gifts. It was his operetta *Der Zigeunerbaron*.

In 1883 Johann had visited Budapest with his wife. There he met the Hungarian novelist Maurus Jókai, who suggested a fetching idea for an operetta: the love-affair of a dispossessed Hungarian grandee for a gypsy. Jókai elaborated the theme for Strauss. As a boy, Sandov is taken from his ancestral home. When he returns many years later he finds the castle overrun with gypsies. He falls in love with one of the gypsy girls—and the story is launched.

As Strauss heard Jókai outline this plot, his eyes gleamed. How familiar he was with the attraction always exerted for the Viennese by the romantic Hungarian gypsies—by the free spirit, the impetuosity and the pride that contrasted so remarkably with their own softer natures! In this plot Strauss realized at once that he had found his new libretto, one capable of firing his inspiration in just the way that *Die Fledermaus* had done many years before.

Soon the libretto was written—not by Jókai but by a journalist named Schnitzer; and Strauss went ahead rapidly on the musical score. It was on the eve of his sixtieth birthday, October 24, 1885, that *Der Zigeuner-baron* was produced at the Theater-an-der-Wien. And what a birthday present it was! The ovations were so thunderous that number after number had to be encored, not once, but in some cases twice and three times. So many were repeated that, actually, the operetta was performed three times that night. Particularly acclaimed were the *Schatz* waltzes, which in English are called *My Darling,* or *Treasure,* or *My Destiny.* The Viennese realized that though Strauss might be growing older, his magic had lost none of its potency.

In *Der Zigeunerbaron,* Strauss brought about the union of diverse characters. For the operetta constituted the marriage of the czardas and the waltz, of the Hungarian spirit and the Austrian. Military splendor and (at least in the operetta) military triumph were crowned by love. Here were all the elements to warm the Austrian heart, which—even while the real world was faring badly—could roam at will with gypsy tribes and win imaginary battles.

And in this operetta Strauss had done even more than cheer Vienna: he achieved what the Emperor had been unable to do with all his diplomacy. Painstakingly the Emperor and his ministers had been trying to make one united kingdom out of the dichotomy of Austria and Hungary, to make one realm of the Dual Monarchy. All their efforts had thus far proved fruitless: the fiery Hungarians remained faithful to their own traditions, heritage, and history. But now, in Strauss's operetta, a certain spiritual union had been effected: here Hungarian spirit and Viennese temperament were blended. And in the tremendous success realized by *Der Zigeunerbaron* not only in Vienna but also in Budapest, a new bond of sympathy and understanding was created between the two parts of the realm.

It seemed as if Strauss would never really grow old. As the years advanced, he dyed his gray hair in a futile attempt to cheat time. But in spirit and energy he stayed young. He worked as hard as ever, and produced as richly; neither inspiration nor inventiveness deserted him. Not all the works produced now were successful—indeed, a few operettas after *Der Zigeunerbaron* failed; but in every one there was enough to prove that, at his best, he was still the incomparable master. As a matter of fact, in 1888 he wrote one of his greatest waltzes of all. It was the *Kaiserwalzer,* his expression of congratulations to Emperor Francis Joseph on the fortieth anniversary of his reign—"one of the most beautiful flowers [as William Ritter wrote] that the fantastic tree of Strauss's music has borne."

His idyllically happy marriage with Adele was a chief source of his continued youth and strength. She seemed to understand his every mood, whim, and fancy—and to cater to them. "I never had the feeling I had married an old man," she said later, and meant it. Differences of age did not exist for them. They were one in spirit. With her, he found serenity and peace and happiness.

At a performance of one of his operettas, the two emperors met again—Emperor Francis Joseph and Emperor Johann the Second. "It is strange," Francis Joseph remarked, "that your music, like yourself, never grows older. Why, you haven't changed at all—and I haven't seen you for a long time. I felicitate you on your opera!"

The Emperor had called the operetta an "opera"— almost as if he had been able to penetrate into the deepest recesses of Strauss's heart! For Strauss had lately been dreaming of turning his creative gifts into a more serious channel. He wanted to leave a permanent legacy before he died; in short, he wanted to write a great serious opera. He set to work, and composed *Ritter Pasman*. The Vienna Court Opera presented it lavishly, with an all-star cast, expensive mountings, and numerous rehearsals at which painstaking attention was devoted to every detail. But, though the work had an enthusiastic reception and enjoyed a moderate success, it remains one of Strauss's poorer works—stilted, artificial, *operatic*. It was not the *real* Johann Strauss, but someone masquerading in pompous clothes. No, Johann Strauss's legacy to the world was still his wonderful operettas and waltzes, the kinds of music that had from the first completely expressed his personality. Eduard Hanslick wrote truly of *Ritter Pasman:* "What we miss in this higher sphere is not the accomplished man of taste and the first-class musician—but simply our beloved Johann Strauss."

Then, in 1894, came the second coda, when Strauss's achievements were reviewed in honor of the fiftieth anniversary of his career. Fifty years of waltzes! Fifty years of an uninterrupted musical reign! It was really incredible! From Berlin, from Hamburg, from Petersburg, even from far-off America there came congratulatory words. Musical societies in America sent him a silver loving-cup with fifty silver leaves on it, each leaf engraved with the title of a Strauss work. Music-lovers in Russia sent him a floral wreath. In many capitals of Europe concerts celebrated the event.

But in Vienna especially was there festivity and celebration. For an entire week the city gave itself up to rejoicing. At concert after concert (some directed by Eduard, others by Johann), Strauss's life-work was summarized from his first waltz to his latest. On October 14, there was a concert in the Music Hall directed by Johann himself; that evening Eduard directed a Promenade concert. On the following day—exactly fifty years since Johann Strauss had made his memorable debut at Dommayer's Casino—the Haupttheater presented a ballet accompanied by a score compounded from Strauss's most famous melodies. Late that night, a brilliant torch-parade wound through the streets, with thousands of Viennese participating.

At the final concert, Johann Strauss made his farewell speech to his public. It expressed not only his own gratitude to Vienna and the Viennese, but also the sentiments of every artist who lived in Vienna, worked in Vienna, and derived his inspiration from that city.

"If it is true that I have talent," Johann said, "I owe it above everything else to my beloved city, Vienna. . . . In her soil is rooted my whole strength, in her air float the melodies which my ear has caught, my heart has drunk in, and my hand has written down. . . . My Vienna, the city of Song and Spirit, who sets the boy lovingly upon his feet, and upon the mature man ever lavishes her sympathies. . . . Vienna, the city of beautiful women who inspire and bewitch the artist. . . . Vienna, the heart of our beautiful, God-blessed Austria, the golden Empire!"

E.C

CHAPTER XXVI

"The Sun Must Set"

ON MAY 22, 1899, STRAUSS WAS CONDUCTING the overture to *Die Fledermaus*. As happened frequently when
he conducted, he sweated profusely. He went home, his
clothes wet with perspiration. Then, after a thorough
rub-down and a change of clothing, he played cards with
some friends.

A slight cold followed. Strauss did not take it very

seriously, however. He continued to work hard on a ballet, *Aschenbrödl* (Cinderella), and he attended a public fête. But the cold got worse, and he had to take to bed because of a high fever.

Within a few days, his illness had turned to double pneumonia, and for the first time his physician, Dr. Notnagle, showed deep concern. In spite of his efforts, the patient, though comfortable, did not improve; on the contrary, he grew worse. His mind seemed to be slipping. He succumbed to hallucinations, imagining that the painted figures on his bedroom door were characters from his many operettas, who had come into his room to meet him. On the first of June he suddenly sat up in his bed and in his delirium sang the popular song which his teacher, Drechsler, had written:

> *Sweet little brother! Sweet little brother!*
> *You mustn't be angry with me!*
> *The sun is still shining so brightly—*
> *Alas! how soon it must set!*

From that day on, Adele remained at Johann's side, comforting him with the cool caress of her hand on his burning forehead. She spoke to him gently, trying somehow to assuage his tortured dreams. Pathetically she tried to pierce through the fog of his delirium; and two days later she was successful. Suddenly Strauss's clarity of mind returned, and he was himself again. He picked up Adele's hand and kissed it.

"But, Johann, you must sleep a little."

"There's plenty of time for sleeping," he whispered.

"Sleep will come soon enough." He knew he was dying. . . .

At four-fifteen of the same day, June 3, he fell asleep. His face suddenly acquired a touch of spirituality, as if he had found peace and rest. The doctor felt his pulse, then gently put down Johann's hand.

"Frau Strauss," he said to Adele, "the sun has set."

That afternoon there was a concert at the Volksgarten. Toward its end a messenger rushed breathlessly to the stand to deliver a note. The conductor read it and turned to face the audience.

"Ladies and gentlemen—" he began.

The babble of the audience dissipated into silence. The conductor, hardly trusting his voice, quickly moistened his lips with the tip of his tongue. "Ladies and gentlemen," he said again, "our beloved Schani is dead."

And before they had fully comprehended the news, he had turned around and lifted his bow. *Pianissimo* the orchestra played *The Blue Danube*.

It was June 6, 1899. Vienna was bowed by sorrow. The houses along the streets leading to the cemetery were draped in black. Dimmed lanterns contributed a spectral note. Everywhere there were drawn faces, as though the city's loss were a personal loss to each and every citizen. The funeral procession passed majestically through streets lined with mourners. The hearse was followed—just as the elder Strauss's had been—by a mourner carrying a silken cushion on which rested the composer's violin. The cortège paused at the church in

the Dorotheagasse, and here the funeral service was held.
Then the procession continued, past the Opera House, to
the door of the Gesellschaft der Musikfreunde, where
speeches were made by some of Vienna's most eminent
musicians. Finally, the body was carried to the Central
Cemetery, to be laid to rest near two other great musicians: Schubert and Brahms. Over the grave more
speeches were delivered, more tears shed. The Choral
Society of Vienna sang Brahms's *Farewell!*

And Vienna wept, for it had lost its best-loved son. It
wept because it knew that in losing Johann Strauss it
had lost a part of itself. As one poet, Max Heyck, put it:

> *What man is, without strength,*
> *What fruit is, without juice,*
> *What a tree is, without leaves,*
> *What summer is, without rain,*
> *What heaven is, without blue . . .*
> *This is Vienna without Johann Strauss!*

Vienna had lost a part of itself which it was never
again to recover.

Though Johann Strauss was dead, his orchestra remained living—for a brief while, at any rate. Eduard
continued to direct it, both in and out of Vienna. In
October, 1900, he brought the orchestra to the United
States for an extensive tour that covered eighty-one cities
and during which 106 concerts were given. On February
12, 1901, the Strauss orchestra was heard for the last
time—at a ball in New York. The following morning,

Eduard gathered the men to tell them that he was disbanding the ensemble; he was ill (his conducting hand pained him acutely) and he must take a rest. Thus, in New York, the orchestra which Father Strauss had founded in Vienna seventy-six years earlier quietly passed out of existence. Returning to Vienna, Eduard lived in semi-retirement, wrote a volume of memoirs, and died in 1916.

Adele Strauss, Johann's wife, lived in complete seclusion in her home in the Igelgasse (renamed the Johann-Straussgasse). There the writer of this book met her, a year before her death in the spring of 1930. Modest and unpretentious, she seemed to be living entirely in the world of memories, in the glamorous past. And how eloquently she talked of her wonderful Johann. . . .

There is a third Johann Strauss. He is still alive; in 1934 he visited the United States. Son of Eduard and nephew of the composer of *The Blue Danube,* he too conducts and writes waltzes; but it cannot be said that he has inherited the Strauss genius.

However, even if no real Strauss was left to carry on the light-music tradition of Vienna, there were others aplenty to do so: Oskar Straus (who, with one s only, is no relation), Leo Fall, Emerich Kálmán, and—most famous and beloved of all—Franz Lehár. These men, too, proved themselves able to write infectious waltz music with the throb of Vienna in it, to compose operettas that carry us away to enchanted worlds on the wings of song. Lehár's operetta, *The Merry Widow,* with its intoxicating waltz, was a worthy successor to *Die Fledermaus.*

But suddenly the waltz comes to an abrupt close. Dancing feet take to marching, and the make-believe kingdom of the operetta turns into a place of thundering guns and bleeding bodies. It is 1914, and in a small town in Serbia an Austrian archduke is assassinated. . . .

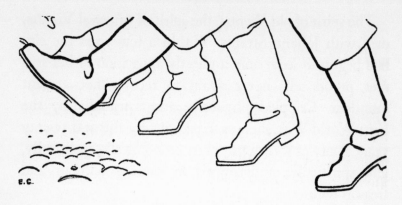

Vienna, City of Sorrow

IT IS SYMBOLIC that Johann Strauss should have died in 1899. The 19th century was drawing to a close, and with it an entire epoch. At Strauss's death, wrote Wallauschek, "the whole musical physiognomy of old Vienna was laid to rest." This was true. Though brilliant composers like Lehár were to continue the city's tradition of light music, and Mahler and Schönberg its serious, Johann Strauss was the last of the Viennese musical giants. With him passed the two-century-old musical glory of a musical city. One could say even more than this, as did a court official in Vienna when he remarked that "the Emperor Francis Joseph reigned until the death of Johann Strauss." Actually, the Emperor's reign continued until 1916, but his real day may be said to have closed with the twilight of the century; thereafter he seemed to be only marking time, awaiting the inevitable end of the Hapsburgs.

The spirit of old Vienna, the spirit of Imperial Vienna, died with Johann Strauss. Within a few years the city had begun to seem only a ghostly apparition of her former proud self, never again to recover her ancient grandeur. Crippled physically and spiritually by the First World War, she was to become, for the next twenty years, a city of sorrow, stricken economically, politically, and spiritually, undermined by enmity without and treason within.

In February 1938, the city died officially. At the end of that month, Nazi troops entered Austria and annexed the country to the Third Reich. In Vienna the Nazi swastika supplanted the red-and-white flag of the Austrian Republic. Banished now were free culture, free art. The goose-step replaced the light-hearted waltz; the military march drowned out the music of Johann Strauss; and the last of Vienna's noble creative spirits were either killed or thrown into concentration camps— unless they were fortunate enough to escape to freer countries.

But who knows? Perhaps out of its trials and sufferings there will some day emerge a new, free, democratic Vienna; a greater and nobler Vienna; a city still of charm and grace and culture, but a city also of free men and women. And when that day comes, perhaps another Johann Strauss will arise to embody the spirit and soul of the new city in music as deathless and as inspired as the waltzes of old.

APPENDICES

Bibliographical Note

Glossary

The Works of Johann Strauss, Jr.

The Music of Johann Strauss, Jr. on Records

Strauss Themes

Strauss Family Chart

The World the Strausses Lived In

BIBLIOGRAPHICAL NOTE

No FORMAL BIBLIOGRAPHY can be printed for this life of Johann Strauss, since there are—in print—virtually no books on him in English. But the reader may find in a public library some recent works, now out of print: H. E. Jacob's *Johann Strauss, Father and Son* (Greystone, 1940), Ada B. Teetgen's *Waltz Kings of Old Vienna* (Dutton, 1939), and David Ewen's *Wine, Women and Waltz* (Sears, 1933). The author has found some of his material in an Austrian biography, not translated into English: Ernst Decsey's *Johann Strauss* (Vienna, 1922). Most of his material, however, was gathered during visits to Vienna before the present war. It was there, also, that the Opus List beginning on page 175 was obtained; reprinted here from Viennese sources, it is (so far as the author knows) the only complete and accurate list of Strauss's works to be found in any American book.

Grateful acknowledgment is made to Mrs. Elizabeth C. Moore for the editing of the text and for the preparation of the music extracts, the lists of works and of records, the table called "The World the Strausses Lived In," the Strauss family chart, and the Index.

GLOSSARY

The text of this book contains a number of German phrases that the author found it impracticable to translate there: names of café-houses and other places in Vienna, titles of musical works, and so forth. Some of these can hardly be translated, because rendering them literally into English would not convey the meaning they had for the Viennese of the period. As for the translatable terms, many of the music titles will be found translated in the Index; other terms are given below. The reader should bear in mind that a phrase used as the name of a café-house is often understood to have the words "At the Sign of" before the name itself—for instance, *Zum Roten Hahn* means "At the Sign of the Red Hen"— since the house took its name from the picture on the sign hanging over the door.

Blaue Flasche—The Blue Flask (or Bottle)
Gesellschaft der Musikfreunde—Society of the Friends of Music
Goldene Birne—The Golden Pear
Goldenen Eule—The Golden Owl
Goldenes Lamm—The Golden Lamb
Goldnen Rebhuhn—The Golden Partridge
Grünen Thore—The Green Door
Grüner Zeisig—The Green Canary
Guten Hirt—The Good Shepherd
Hirschenhaus—The House of the Stag (or Deer)
Kapellmeister—the first violin of an orchestra, who in some cases
    was also its conductor

Roten Hahn—The Red Hen

Schnitzel—meat cutlets, often called Wienerschnitzel

Schottengymnasium—the "gymnasium" part of this phrase does not have our sense, but in Austria and Germany means a secondary school

Siebenkurfürsten—The Seven Electors

Stadt Belgrad—The City of Belgrade

Zwei Tauben—The Two Doves

THE WORKS OF JOHANN STRAUSS, JR.

followed by a list of works composed in collaboration with his brothers

NOTE—*Titles set in heavy type are those of works for which recordings can be bought. See record list beginning on page 186.*

OPERETTAS

Indigo and the Forty Thieves, Feb. 10, 1871
Roman Carnival, March 1, 1873
Die Fledermaus (The Bat), April 5, 1874
Cagliostro, Feb. 27, 1875
Prince Methusaleh, Jan. 3, 1877
The Blind Cow, Dec. 18, 1878
The Queen's Lace Handkerchief, Oct. 1, 1880

The Merry War, Nov. 25, 1881
A Night in Venice, Oct. 3, 1883
The Gypsy Baron, Oct. 24, 1885
Simplizius, Dec. 17, 1887
Ritter Pasman, Jan. 1, 1892
Ninetta, Jan. 10, 1893
Jabuka, Oct. 12, 1894
Waldmeister, Dec. 4, 1895
The Goddess of Reason, March 13, 1897

WALTZES, POLKAS, AND OTHER DANCE MUSIC

in order of first performance or of publication

Oct. 15, 1844, at Dommayer's Casino

OPUS
1. Epigrams Waltzes
2. Debut Quadrille
3. Herzenslust Waltzes
4. Gunstwerber Waltzes

OPUS
5. Seraglio Dances
6. Cytherea Quadrille
7. Young Viennese Waltzes

OPUS   1845

8. Patriots' March
9. Amazons' Polka
10. Liebesbrunnen Quadrille
11. Carnival Songs Waltzes
12. Youth's Dreams Waltzes
13. Czech Polka
14. Serb Quadrille
15. Sträusschen Waltzes
16. Elves' Quadrille
17. Jux Polka
18. Berglieder Waltzes
19. Demons' Quadrille
20. Austria March

1846

21. (Jenny) Lind's Songs Waltzes
22. Austrians' Waltzes
23. Pesth Csardas
24. Gypsy Quadrille
25. Zeitgeist Waltzes
26. Fidelio Polka
27. Sanguiniker Waltzes
28. Hopser Polka
29. Odeon Quadrille
30. Zillerthaler Waltzes
31. Quadrille on themes from Balfe's *The Siege of Rochelle*

1847-1849

32. Irene Waltzes
33. Alexandra Quadrille
34. Jovial Waltzes
35. Industry Quadrille

OPUS

36. Architects' Ball Waltzes
37. Wilhelmine Quadrille
38. Bacchus Polka
39. Slav Potpourri
40. Quadrille on themes from Baisselot's *The Queen of Leon*
41. Sängerfahrten
42. Wild Rose Waltzes
43. **Explosions Polka**
44. **Festival Quadrille**
45. Ernte-Tänze Waltzes
46. Martha Quadrille
47. Village Tales Waltzes
48. Seladon Quadrille
49. Festival March
50. Wallachian Songs
51. Marie Quadrille
52. Songs of Freedom Waltzes
53. Annika Quadrille
54. Revolution March
55. Burschenlieder Waltzes
56. Students' March
57. Liguorianer-Seufzer Polka
58. Brünner Natl. Guard March
59. Quadrille on themes from Halévy's *The Attack*
60. Geisselhiebe Polka
61. New Styrian Dances
62. Einheitsklänge Waltzes
63. Sans Souci Quadrille
64. Fantasiebilder Waltzes
65. Nicolai Quadrille in Russian Style
66. D'Waldbuama Waltzes

OPUS   1850

67. Kaiser Franz Josef
    Waltzes
68. Aeolian Harp Waltzes
69. Triumphal March
70. Die Gemütlichen Waltzes
71. Artists' Quadrille
72. Scherzo Polka
73. Frohsinns Spenden Waltzes
74. Lava Stream Waltzes
75. Sophie Quadrille
76. Attack Quadrille
77. Vienna Garrison March
78. Heiligenstadt Rendezvous
    Polka
79. Maxingtänze Waltzes
80. Heski Holki Polka
81. Louisen-Sympathieklänge
    Waltzes
82. Johanniskäferl Waltzes
83. Ottinger Reitermarsch
84. Warsaw Polka
85. Heimatskinder Waltzes
86. Bonvivant Quadrille
87. Aurora-Balltänze Waltzes
88. Slav Ball Quadrille
89. Hirtenspiele
90. Orakelsprüche Waltzes
91. Hermann Polka
92. Masquerade Quadrille
93. Kaiserjäger March
94. Rhadamantusklänge
    Waltzes
95. Idyl Waltzes
96. Viribus unitis March
97. Gambrinus Dances

OPUS

98. Promenade Quadrille
99. Frauenkäferin Waltzes
100. Vöslauer Polka
101. Mephistos Höllenrufe
    Waltzes
102. Albion Polka

1851

103. Vivant Quadrille
104. Windsor Waltzes
105. Five Paragraphs from the
    Waltz Codex—Waltzes

1852

106. Harmony Polka
107. Grand Duke March
108. Unzertrennlichen Waltzes
109. Tête-à-tête Quadrille
110. Electromagnetic Polka
111. Flower Festival Polka
112. Quadrille on Verdi Melo-
    dies
113. Saxon Cuirassiers' March
114. **Liebeslieder Waltzes**
115. Vienna Jubilee Greeting
    March
116. Court Ball Quadrille
117. Army Polka
118. Lockvögel Waltzes
119. Folk-Song Waltzes
120. Nocturne Quadrille
121. Zehner Polka
122. Indra Quadrille
123. Satanella Quadrille

The Works of Johann Strauss, Jr.

124. Satanella Polka
125. Phönix-Schwingen Waltzes
126. Rettungs-Jubelmarsch
127. Freudengruss Polka
128. Solon Sayings Waltzes
129. Motor Quadrille
130. Aesculapius Polka
131. Vienna Punch Songs
     Waltzes
132. Violet Polka
133. Carrousel March
134. Tanzi-Bäri Polka
135. Banquet Quadrille
136. Nuptial Toast Waltzes
137. Neuhauser Polka
138. Pepita Polka
139. Crown March
140. Knallkügerin Waltzes
141. Waves and Billows Waltzes
142. Wiedersehen Polka
143. Snowdrop Waltzes
144. La Viennoise Polka-
     Mazurka
145. Bürgerball Polka
146. Novellen Waltzes
147. Muses Polka

1854

148. Acoustics Waltzes
149. Erzherzog-Wilhelm-Genes-
     ungs March
150. **Tales of the Ball Waltzes**
151. Elise Polka
152. Carnival Sights Quadrille
153. Quadrille on themes from

OPUS

Meyerbeer's *L'Etoile du Nord*

154. Myrtle Wreath Waltzes
155. Haute-volée Polka
156. Napoleon March
157. Nachtfalter Waltzes
158. Alliance March
159. **Fast Mail Polka**
160. Ella Polka

1855

161. Panacea Songs Waltzes
162. Souvenir Polka
163. Glossen Waltzes
164. Sirens Waltzes
165. Aurora Polka
166. Handels-Elite Quadrille
167. We Live But Once Waltzes
168. Leopoldstadt Polka
169. Bijouterie Quadrille
170. Night Violets Polka-
     Mazurka
171. Freudensalven Waltzes
172. Thoughts from the Alps
     Waltzes
173. Maria Taglioni Polka
174. Butterfly Polka-Mazurka

1856

175. Fast Pulse Waltzes
176. Armenball Polka
177. Jurists' Ball Dances
178. Sans Souci Polka
179. Farewell Waltzes
180. Libellen Waltzes

OPUS

181. Grand Duchess Alexandra Waltzes
182. L'Inconnue Polka
183. Coronation March

1857

184. Coronation Waltzes
185. Strelna Terrace Quadrille
186. Demi-Fortune Polka
187. Bagatelle Polka-Mazurka
188. Herzel Polka
189. **Paroxysm Waltzes**
190. Etwas kleines Polka
191. Controversy Waltzes
192. Wien mein Sinn Waltzes
193. Phenomena Waltzes
194. La Berceuse Quadrille
195. **Telegraph Messages Waltzes**
196. Olga Polka
197. Spleen Polka-Mazurka
198. Alexandria Polka
199. Le Beau-monde Quadrille

1858

200. Souvenir of Nizza Waltzes
201. Artists' Quadrille
202. L'Enfantillage Polka
203. Hellenes Polka
204. Vibration Waltzes
205. Extravaganten Waltzes
206. Concordia Polka-Mazurka
207. Cycloids Waltzes
208. Juxbrüder Waltzes
209. Spirals Waltzes
210. Farewell to St. Petersburg Waltzes

OPUS

211. Champagne Polka
212. Prince Bariatinsky March
213. Bonbon Polka
214. **Tritsch-Tratsch Polka**

1859

215. Gedankenflug Waltzes
216. Hell und voll Waltzes
217. La Favorite Polka
218. Irrlichter Waltzes
219. Aurora Ball Polka
220. German Waltzes
221. **Promotion Waltzes**
222. Nightingale Polka
223. Flywheels Waltzes
224. Dinorah Quadrille
225. Greeting to Vienna Polka
226. Kobold Polka-Mazurka
227. Travel Adventures Waltzes
228. Niko Polka
229. Hunters' Polka

1860

230. Kammerball Polka
231. Drollery Polka
232. Lebenswecker Waltzes
233. Sentence Waltzes
234. **Acceleration Waltzes**
235. Immer heiterer Waltzes
236. Orpheus Quadrille
237. Pigeon Post Polka
238. Parisians Polka
239. Polka-Mazurka (champêtre)
240. Maskenzug Polka

OPUS   1860

241. Fantasieblümchen Polka-
Mazurka
242. Bijoux Polka
243. Romanze I
244. Diabolin Polka

1861

245. Thermen Waltzes
246. Rokonhangok Polka
247. Grillenbanner Waltzes
248. Camellia Polka
249. Hesperus Polka
250. Wahlstimmen Waltzes
251. Klangfiguren Waltzes
252. Dividends Waltzes
253. Schwärmereien Concert
Waltzes
254. New Melodies Quadrille
(on themes from Italian
operas)

1862

255. Romanze II and St. Petersburg Quadrille
256. Violet Mazurka on Russian
themes
257. **Perpetuum mobile**
258. Sekunden Polka
259. Chansonette Quadrille on
French themes
260. Furioso Polka
261. First Cure Waltzes
262. Kolonnen Waltzes
263. Students' Polka
264. Patroness Waltzes
265. **Motor Waltzes**

OPUS

266. Lucifer Polka
267. Concurrence Waltzes
268. Vienna Chronicle Waltzes
269. Demolition Polka
270. Carnival Messages Waltzes
271. Bluette Polka
272. Quadrille on themes from
Verdi's *Masked Ball*

1863

273. Zeitartikel Waltzes
274. Patriots' Polka
275. Lieder Quadrille on favorite
themes
276. Bauern Polka
277. Invitation to the Polka-
Mazurka
278. New Life Polka

1864

279. **Morning Journals Waltzes**
280. Jurists' Ball Polka
281. Excursion Train Polka
282. Gut bürgerlich Polka
283. Season Quadrille
284. German War March
285. Studentenlust Waltzes
286. Patroness Polka
287. Verbrüderungsmarsch
288. Newa Polka
289. **Persian March**
290. Quadrille on French airs
291. 's gibt nur a Kaiserstadt, 's
gibt nur a Wien Polka
292. From the Mountains
Waltzes

OPUS   1865

293. Feuilleton Waltzes
294. Process Polka
295. Bürgersinn Waltzes
296. Episode Polka
297. **Electrofor Polka**
298. Court Ball Waltzes
299. Quadrille on themes from Meyerbeer's *L'Africana*
300. Flugschriften Waltzes
301. Kreuzfidel Polka
302. Zeitlose Polka
303. Bal champêtre Quadrille
304. Children's Play Polka

1866

305. Damenspende Polka
306. Burgerweisen Waltzes
307. **Vienna Bonbons Waltzes**
308. Par force Polka
309. Sylven Polka
310. Tändelei Polka-Mazurka
311. Express Polka
312. Fairy-tales Waltzes
313. Wildfire Polka

1867

314. **The Beautiful Blue Danube Waltzes**
315. Lob der Frauen Polka-Mazurka
316. **Artists' Life Waltzes**
317. Postillon d'amour Polka
318. Telegram Waltzes
319. Leichtes Blut Polka
320. Figaro Polka

OPUS   1868

321. Publicists Waltzes
322. Town and Country Polka-Mazurka
323. Ein Herz ein Sinn Polka-Mazurka
324. **Thunder and Lightning Polka**
325. **Tales from the Vienna Woods Waltzes**
326. Freikugeln Polka
327. Day of Happiness Quadrille
328. Sängerlust Polka
329. Covent Garden Memories Waltzes

1869

330. Fata morgana Polka-Mazurka
331. Illustrations Waltzes
332. Eljen a Magyar Polka
333. **Wine, Woman, and Song Waltzes**
334. Königslieder Waltzes
335. **Egyptian March**

1870-1872

336. Im Pawlowskwalde Polka
337. From the Bourse Polka
338. Slovianka Quadrille on Russian Airs
339. Louischen Polka
340. Joy of Living Waltzes
341. Festival Quadrille on English Airs
342. **New Vienna Waltzes**
343. Schal Polka (from *Indigo*)

OPUS 1870-1872

344. *Indigo* Quadrille
345. Auf freiem Fusse Polka
346. **Thousand and One Nights Waltzes**
347. From Home Polka-Mazurka
348. Im Sturmschritt Polka (from *Indigo*)
349. **"Indigo" March**
350. Lustiger Rath Polka
351. Bayadere Polka (from *Indigo*)
352. Festival Polonaise for large orchestra
353. Russian March Fantasie
354. **Vienna Blood Waltzes**
355. In a Russian Village Fantasie for large orchestra
356. From Danube Shores Polka (from *Roman Carnival*)
357. Carnival Scenes Waltzes
358. Nimm sie hin Polka
359. Greeting from Austria Polka-Mazurka

1873-1877

360. Rotunda Quadrille
361. **Bei uns z'Haus**
362. *Fledermaus* Polka
363. *Fledermaus* Quadrille
364. **Citronen Waltzes** (Where the Citrons Bloom)
365. Tik-tak Polka
366. Moldau Polka (from *Die Fledermaus*)

OPUS

367. **Du und Du Waltzes** (*Fledermaus*)
368. Glücklich ist Polka-Mazurka (*Fledermaus*)
369. *Cagliostro* Quadrille
370. **"Cagliostro" Waltzes**
371. Hoch Oesterreich March (*Cagliostro*)
372. Bitte schön Polka (*Cagliostro*)
373. At the Hunt Polka (*Cagliostro*)
374. Light and Shadow Polka (*Cagliostro*)
375. O Lovely May Waltzes (*Prince Methusaleh*)
376. *Methusaleh* Quadrille
377. I-Tipferl Polka (*Methusaleh*)
378. Bandits Galop Polka (*Methusaleh*)
379. Kriegers Liebschen Polka-Mazurka

1878-1880

380. Ballsträusschen Polka
381. Kennst du mich? Waltzes (from *The Blind Cow*)
382. Parisian Polka (*The Blind Cow*)
383. Nur fort Polka (*The Blind Cow*)
384. Masked Ball Quadrille (*The Blind Cow*)
385. Waldine Polka-Mazurka
386. Frisch heran Polka

387. Ins Zentrum Waltzes
388. **Roses from the South (or Southern Roses) Waltzes**
389. Burschenwanderung Polka for Men's Chorus and Orchestra
390. North Sea Pictures Waltzes
391. Queen's Gavotte (from *The Queen's Lace Handkerchief*)
392. Handkerchief Quadrille (*The Queen's Lace Handkerchief*)
393. Stürmisch in Lieb' und Tanz Polka (*The Queen's Lace Handkerchief*)
394. Liebchen, schwing dich Polka (*The Queen's Lace Handkerchief*)

1881-1894

395. Myrtle Blossoms Waltzes for Men's Chorus and Orchestra
396. Jubilee Festival March for Men's Chorus and Orchestra
397. Merry War March (from *The Merry War*)
398. Frisch ins Feld March
399. Was sich lieb, neckt sich Polka
400. Kiss Waltz (*The Merry War*)
401. Der Klügere gibt nach

Polka-Mazurka (*The Merry War*)
402. Quadrille on themes from *The Merry War*
403. Entweder—oder! Polka (*The Merry War*)
404. Violetta Polka on themes from *The Merry War*
405. North and South Polka-Mazurka (*The Merry War*)
406. Matador March on themes from *The Queen's Lace Handkerchief*
407. Italian Waltzes on themes from *The Merry War*
408. Habsburg hoch March
409. Rasch in der Tat Polka
410. **Voices of Spring Waltzes**
411. **Lagoon Waltzes** on themes from *A Night in Venice*
412. Papacoda Polka on themes from *A Night in Venice*
413. So ängstlich sind wir nicht Galop on themes from *A Night in Venice*
414. The Pigeons of St. Mark's Polka on themes from *A Night in Venice*
415. Annina Polka-Mazurka on themes from *A Night in Venice*
416. Quadrille on themes from *A Night in Venice*
417. Bridal Parade Polka on

OPUS

464. Herjemineh Polka (from *Waldmeister*)
465. Love and Marriage Polka-Mazurka (*Waldmeister*)
466. Klipp-klapp Galop (*Waldmeister*)
467. Es war so wunderschön March (*Waldmeister*)
468. *Waldmeister* Quadrille

1896-1897

469. Wedding Prelude
470. Deutschmeister Jubilee March
471. Today Is Today Waltzes (from *The Goddess of Reason*)

OPUS

472. Nur nicht mucken Polka (*The Goddess of Reason*)
473. Wo unsre Fahne weht Polka (*The Goddess of Reason*)
474. Hussar Song (*The Goddess of Reason*)
475. Solo Waltzes (*The Goddess of Reason*)
476. Potpourri from *The Goddess of Reason*
477. Elbe Waltzes
478. Aufs Korn! March

1898

479. Klänge aus der Raimundszeit

WITHOUT OPUS NUMBER

Erster Gedanke (First Thought)
Problem
Freiwillige vor! (1887)
Serb March

Einlage der Pauline (*Waldmeister*)
Ein Gstanzl vom Tanzl
Auf zum Tanze

Homage to the Russian Public (Potpourri)

POSTHUMOUS WORKS

Traumbilder, Vols. I and II
Abschieds Waltzes
Ischler Waltzes

Odeon Waltzes (1908)
Aschenbrödel (Cinderella) Ballet

BY JOHANN AND JOSEF STRAUSS

Pizzicato Polka
Hinter den Kulissen Quadrille (1859)

Fatherland March (1859)
Monster Quadrille (1860)

BY JOHANN, JOSEF, AND EDUARD STRAUSS

Trifolien (1865)

Schützen Quadrille (1868)

THE MUSIC OF JOHANN STRAUSS, JR. ON RECORDS

NOTE—The following selected list comprises the best of the Strauss records now available in this country. Foreign recordings—of these or other works by Strauss—are almost unobtainable owing to the war; your dealer will tell you as soon as they are being imported again.

I—COLLECTIONS IN ALBUMS

VICTOR Albums:

DM-445. Album of Strauss Waltzes—Boston Pops, A. Fiedler

Wine, Woman, and Song; Vienna Blood; Artists' Life; Emperor Waltzes; Voices of Spring

DM-665. Four Novelty Waltzes—Boston Pops, Fiedler

Loves of the Poet (by Johann Strauss, III); New Vienna Waltzes; *Cagliostro* Waltzes; Lagoon Waltz (*A Night in Venice*)

EM-1. Strauss Album—Boston Pops, Fiedler

Egyptian March; Persian March; *Indigo* March; *Gypsy Baron* March

DM-262. Music of Johann Strauss—Minneapolis Symphony, Ormandy

The Blue Danube; Acceleration Waltzes; Tales from the Vienna Woods; *Fledermaus* Overture; *Gypsy Baron* Overture

M-561. Viennese Music of Johann Strauss—Vienna Choir Boys, with piano

> Blue Danube; Emperor Waltzes; Pizzicato Polka; Selections from *Die Fledermaus,* Act II; and (by Johann Strauss, Sr.) Radetzky March

DM-907. Three Delightful Waltzes—Vienna Philharmonic, Krauss and Kleiber

> Songs of Love (Liebeslieder); Morning Papers; Du und Du

DC-15. Waltzes of Johann and Josef Strauss—European orchestras, Krauss, Blech, and Kleiber

> Thousand and One Nights; My Darling; Artists' Life; Reminiscences of Vienna; and (by Josef Strauss) Village Swallows

DM-805. Waltzes of Strauss—European orchestras, Walter and Szell

> *Fledermaus* Overture; *Gypsy Baron* Overture; Blue Danube; Emperor

P-14. Strauss Waltzes—by various orchestras

> Blue Danube; Vienna Blood; Artists' Life; Du und Du; Vienna Bonbons

P-7. Famous Waltzes by Strauss—Paramount Theatre Orchestra, London

> Sweetheart (Treasure, My Darling); Southern Roses; selections from the picture *The Great Waltz*

COLUMBIA Albums:

M-389 and M-445. Rediscovered Music of Johann Strauss (2 vols.)—CBS Orchestra, Barlow

> M-389: Seraglio Dances; Explosions Polka; Electrofor Polka; Festival Quadrille; Paroxysm Waltzes
>
> M-445: Motor Waltzes; Ballgeschichten (Tales of the Ball); Telegraph Messages; Champagne Polka; Schnellpost (Fast Mail) Polka

M-364. Strauss Waltzes—Symphony Orchestra, Weingartner and Walter

> Southern Roses; Tales from the Vienna Woods; Thousand and One Nights; Voices of Spring

M-481. Strauss Waltzes by André Kostelanetz

> Blue Danube; Tales from the Vienna Woods; Artists' Life; Voices of Spring; Vienna Life; Emperor

C-13. Strauss Waltzes in Dance Tempo—Al Goodman and Orchestra

> Blue Danube; Vienna Blood; Southern Roses; Wine, Woman, and Song; Tales from the Vienna Woods; Voices of Spring; Emperor; Artists' Life

> (Columbia set C-17 contains Du und Du, and M-494 contains Heut macht die Welt Sonntag)

DECCA Album:

A-318. Strauss Waltzes for Dancing—Harry Horlick and his Orchestra

> Thousand and One Nights; Promotion Waltzes; Bei uns z' Haus; Danube Maidens (*Simplizius*); Lagoon Waltz (*A Night in Venice*); New Vienna Waltzes; Wedding Dance; and (by Strauss, Sr.) Lorelei Rhine Songs

II—SEPARATE RECORDINGS

(some of them not included in any of the albums above)

V11-8580. The Beautiful Blue Danube—N.B.C. Symphony Orchestra, Toscanini

V-11894 ⎫
D-18266 ⎭ Citronen Waltzes (Where the Citrons Bloom)

V-18220. Emperor Waltzes—Philadelphia Orchestra, Ormandy
C 9080-M. *Fledermaus* Overture

D-29015. *Fledermaus* Finale

VII-8579. *Fledermaus,* "Laughing Song" from Act II—Militza Korjus

C 9083-M. *Gypsy Baron* Overture

V-16184. *Gypsy Baron* Selections—John Charles Thomas

V-4435. Perpetuum mobile—Boston Pops, Fiedler

C 9076-M. Perpetuum mobile

V-1757. Pizzicato Polka (by Johann and Josef Strauss)—Minneapolis Orchestra, Ormandy

C 11800-D. Schatz Waltz (My Darling) from *Gypsy Baron*

V-4319. Thunder and Lightning Polka—Boston Pops, Fiedler

C 386-M. Tritsch-Tratsch Polka

D-23034. Vienna Bonbons

STRAUSS THEMES

*A thematic guide to the best-loved works of Johann Strauss, Jr.,
with similar extracts from works by his father
and his brother Josef*

Radetzky March BY JOHANN STRAUSS, SR.

Lorelei-Rheinklänge BY JOHANN STRAUSS, SR.

BY JOHANN STRAUSS, JR.

Acceleration Waltzes, Op. 234

Perpetuum mobile, Op. 257

Morning Journals Waltzes, Op. 279

The Beautiful Blue Danube Waltzes, Op. 314

Artists' Life Waltzes, Op. 316

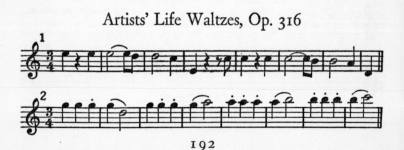

Tales from the Vienna Woods, Op. 325

Wine, Woman, and Song Waltzes, Op. 333

Vienna Blood Waltzes, Op. 354

Du und Du Waltzes
from *Die Fledermaus,* Op. 367

Southern Roses Waltzes, Op. 388

Voices of Spring Waltzes, Op. 410

Schatz Waltz (My Darling, or Treasure) from *The Gypsy Baron,* Op. 418

Emperor Waltzes, Op. 437

Pizzicato Polka BY JOHANN AND JOSEF STRAUSS

Sphärenklänge BY JOSEF STRAUSS

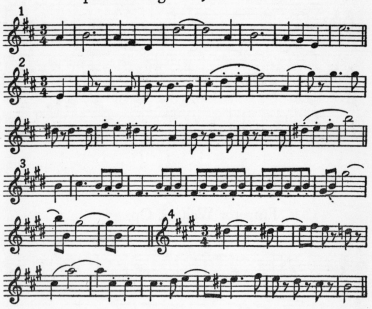

Village Swallows BY JOSEF STRAUSS

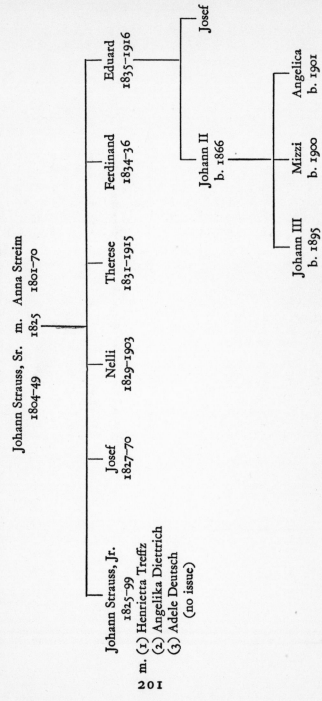

STRAUSS FAMILY CHART

Johann Strauss, Sr.   m.   Anna Streim
1804–49   1825   1801–70

Johann Strauss, Jr.   Josef   Nelli   Therese   Ferdinand   Eduard
1825–99   1827–70   1829–1903   1831–1915   1834–36   1835–1916

m. (1) Henrietta Treffz   Johann II   Josef
   (2) Angelika Diettrich   b. 1866
   (3) Adele Deutsch
      (no issue)

                                                          Johann III   Mizzi   Angelica
                                                          b. 1895   b. 1900   b. 1901

THE WORLD THE STRAUSSES LIVED IN

THE STRAUSS FAMILY	MUSICAL EVENTS	WORLD EVENTS
1804 Johann Strauss the elder born on March 14.	1804 Born: Mikhail Glinka.	1804 Died: Kant, Alexander Hamilton. Born: Disraeli and Hawthorne.
	1805 Died: Boccherini.	1805 Died: Nelson (at Trafalgar), Schiller. Born: Mazzini, Hans Christian Andersen.
		1807 Born: Longfellow, Whittier, Garibaldi, R. E. Lee, Louis Agassiz.
	1809 Died: Haydn. Born: Mendelssohn.	1809 Born: Lincoln, Darwin, Gladstone, Tennyson, Poe, Kit Carson, Holmes.
	1810 Born: Chopin and Schumann.	1810 Born: Cavour, Musset, Barnum.
	1811 B.—Liszt.	1811 B.—Thackeray, Sumner, Greeley.
	1813 B.—Verdi and Wagner.	1813 B.—Livingstone, Frémont, Stephen A. Douglas.
1818 Strauss, aged 14, plays at the Sperl under Pamer.	1818 B.—Gounod.	1818 D.—George Rogers Clark, Paul Revere, Light-Horse Harry Lee.
1819 Strauss, aged 15, joins forces with Lanner, aged 18.	1819 B.—Offenbach, Clara Wieck (Schumann). Weber composes the *Invitation to the Dance*.	1819 B.—Queen Victoria, Whitman, Julia Ward Howe, George Eliot, Ruskin, Lowell, Kingsley. *Rip Van Winkle* and *Ivanhoe* published.

1820 B.—Jenny Lind, Vieuxtemps.	1820 D.—Boone, Decatur. B.—Florence Nightingale, Wm. T. Sherman.

1822 B.—César Franck.	1822 D.—Shelley. B.—Pasteur, Grant, Matthew Arnold.

1824 B.—Smetana, Bruckner.	1824 D.—Byron. B.—Stonewall Jackson.

1825 Strauss breaks with Lanner, starts his own orchestra, and marries. First son, Johann, born Oct. 25.

1825 First performance of Italian opera in America: *The Barber of Seville,* by the Garcías in N. Y. C.	1825 D.—Eli Whitney. B.—T. H. Huxley. Erie Canal opened. J. Q. Adams inaugurated.

1826 D.—Weber. B.—Stephen Foster.	1826 D. (July 4)—Jefferson, John Adams.

1827 Josef Strauss born.

1827 D.—Beethoven. Schubert writes E flat Trio, begins *Winterreise.*	1827 D.—Volta, Blake, Laplace. B.—Lister. Great naval battle of Navarino.

1828 Schubert dies, shortly before the first perf. of his great Symphony #7 in C major.	1828 B.—Tolstoi, Ibsen, Verne, Meredith, D. G. Rossetti. Publication of Webster's *American Dictionary,* first ed.

1829 Daughter Nelli born. (Lanner is appointed Musical Director of Court balls.)

1829 B.—Rubinstein. World première of Rossini's *William Tell.* Mendelssohn revives *Matthew Passion.*	1829 D.—John Jay. Andrew Jackson's first inauguration.

1830 Strauss has his own orchestra of 200 musicians playing at the Sperl.

1830 B.—Goldmark, Bülow, Leschetizky. World prems. of Berlioz, *Fantastic Symphony;* Chopin, E minor Concerto.	1830 B.—Emperor Francis Joseph. Popular revolts in Europe. Paris Revolution brings Louis Philippe to throne.

THE STRAUSS FAMILY	MUSICAL EVENTS	WORLD EVENTS
1831 Daughter Therese born.	1831 World prems. of Bellini's *Norma* and *Sonnambula*, Hérold's *Zampa*. In Boston, *America* is first sung.	1831 D.—Monroe. McCormick invents his reaper. First steam-drawn trains in U.S.—Albany to Schenectady.
1832 Strauss's orchestra is heard by Wagner (aged 19) on a visit to Vienna.	1832 Prems. of *Hebrides* and *Calm Sea* Overtures and *Reformation* Symphony by Mendelssohn. Schumann lames hand.	1832 D.—Goethe. Parliamentary Reform Act passed in Britain. In U.S., cholera epidemic, Black Hawk War.
	1833 B.—Brahms, Borodin.	1833 B.—Edwin Booth, "Chinese" Gordon, L. M. Alcott. Jackson's 2d inauguration. He closes Bank of United States.
1834 Strauss takes orchestra to Berlin and plays before Friedrich Wilhelm III. Son Ferdinand born.	1834 D.—Halévy, Boïeldieu. B.—Ponchielli.	1834 D.—Lamb, Coleridge. B.—Whistler, Du Maurier, Mendeléyev. In U.S., financial panic begins long inflation.
1835 Strauss and his orchestra on concert tour of western Germany. Son Eduard born.	1835 D.—Bellini. B.—Saint-Saëns, Wieniawski, Theodore Thomas. World prem. of Donizetti's *Lucia*.	1835 D.—John Marshall. B.—Mark Twain, Carnegie, Gaboriau. Colt invents revolver. Texas proclaims independence from Mexico.
1836 With his orchestra, Strauss tours western Germany, Holland, Belgium. Johann begins his four years at Schottengymnasium.	1836 Prems. of Meyerbeer's *Huguenots*, Glinka's *A Life for the Tsar*, Mendelssohn's *St. Paul*.	1836 D.—Burr, Crockett, Madison. Siege of the Alamo. Republic of Texas set up. *Pickwick Papers* published.
1837 Strauss takes orchestra to Paris; plays for Louis Philippe and King	1837 B.—Balakirev, Waldteufel. World prem. Berlioz' *Requiem*. Schu-	1837 B.—Conrad, Swinburne, Howells. Victoria succeeds to throne. In U.S.

of the Belgians. Dedicates new waltz *Der Diamant* to Berlioz.

1838 Takes orchestra to England for Coronation ceremonies. Then on tour in Scotland and Ireland.

1839 Early in the year Strauss returns ill, does not recover for months.

1840 Johann leaves school for lessons with Drexler; begins study of composition. Strauss leaves his family permanently.

1843 Strauss, Sr., is appointed conductor of First Militia Regt. band; Lanner; of 2d Regt. band. Lanner dies; Johann is appointed to his place as band conductor.

---

mann engaged to Clara Wieck. Wagner conducts at Königsberg and Riga.

1838 B.—Bizet, Bruch. Jenny Lind's debut, Stockholm. World prem. of Berlioz' *Benvenuto Cellini.*

1839 B.—Mussorgsky. Schumann rediscovers Schubert's Symphony #7 in C and Mendelssohn conducts it in Leipzig. Wagner visits London and Paris.

1840 D.—Paganini. B.—Tchaikovsky. The Schumann marriage. World prems. of Donizetti's *Favorita* and *Daughter of the Regiment.*

1841 B.—Dvořák, Chabrier. World prem. of Schumann's *Spring Symphony.* American prem. of Beethoven's 5th, Boston.

1843 B.—Grieg, Patti, Richter. Leipzig Conservatory opens, headed by Mendelssohn. Wagner appointed Court opera conductor, Leipzig, produces *The Flying Dutchman.*

---

financial panic; first iron ship built. *Oliver Twist* published.

1838 B.—John Hay, Gambetta, Henry Irving. Victoria crowned, June 28. S.S. *Great Western* makes historic 15-day crossing, Bristol-N.Y.C.

1839 B.—Custer, Cézanne, Henry George. Victoria marries Albert. Daguerre invents photography. *Nicholas Nickleby* published.

1840 B.—Daudet, Rodin, Monet, Zola, Hardy. Penny postage introduced in Britain. Napoleon's body brought from St. Helena for Paris entombment.

1841 B.—Edward VII, Stanley, Clemenceau. *Punch* starts publication. Emerson's *Essays* pub. Longfellow writes "Excelsior."

1843 D.—F. S. Key, Noah Webster. Bunker Hill Monument completed. Publ. of *Martin Chuzzlewit* and *A Christmas Carol,* "The Gold Bug," and "Ben Bolt."

THE STRAUSS FAMILY	MUSICAL EVENTS	WORLD EVENTS
1844 Strauss, Sr., divorced by wife. Johann applies for license to conduct his own orchestra. Debut at Dommayer's, Oct. 15.	1844 B.—Sarasate and Rimsky-Korsakov. World prems. Verdi's *Ernani*, Wagner's *Faust* Overture, Schumann Pf. Quartet, Op. 47.	1844 B.—Bernhardt, Modjeska, Verlaine, A. France. Morse sends first telegraph message, Washington to Baltimore.
	1847 D.—Mendelssohn. World prem. of Schumann's Piano Concerto, played by Clara.	1847 B.—Edison, A. G. Bell, Hindenburg. *Jane Eyre*, *Wuthering Heights*, *Evangeline*, published.
1848 Strauss, Sr., writes the *Radetzky* and other marches for Imperial cause during Austrian revolution. Johann composes for the revolutionists.	1848 D.—Donizetti. Wagner joins Dresden revolutionary organization. Epoch of military marches begins in Austria.	1848 B.—Gauguin, St.-Gaudens. Revolutions in Europe (Hungary, Italy, Bavaria, Vienna, Paris). Francis Joseph becomes Emperor; Louis Napoleon, French president.
1849 Strauss plays in London; home in July. Dies, Sept. 25. His orchestra merges with Johann's.	1849 D.—Chopin. Wagner exiled to Switzerland. Prems. Meyerbeer's *Le Prophète*, Nicolai's *Merry Wives of Windsor*.	1849 D.—Poe, Anne Brontë. B.—Burbank, Pavlov. Zachary Taylor inaugurated. Gold Rush to California. *David Copperfield* published.
1854 Johann Strauss begins his ten years of summer seasons in Russia. Josef now deputizes for him occasionally.	1854 B.—Humperdinck, Moszkowski. Schumann goes insane. The N. Y. Academy of Music opens with *Norma*.	1854 Crimean War begins; Charge of Light Brigade, Balaklava. Perry opens the ports of Japan. *Uncle Tom's Cabin* published.
	1858 Première of Offenbach's *Orphée aux enfers*.	1858 B.—T. Roosevelt, Booker Washington.
1859 Eduard becomes a conductor of Strauss orchestras, along with Jo-	1859 Prems., Gounod's *Faust*, Brahms's 1st Piano Concerto. Patti's operatic	1859 D.—Metternich, Macaulay. John Brown attacks Harpers Ferry;

hann and Josef, and begins to compose.	debut, N.Y.C. *Dixie* is first sung, N.Y.C.	is hanged. *A Tale of Two Cities, The Origin of Species* published.
1862 Johann Strauss marries Henrietta Treffz. Builds Hietzing villa.	1862 B.—Debussy, Delius, W. Damrosch. Prem. Verdi's *La Forza del destino.* First concert of Thomas's Orchestra, N.Y.C.	1862 Fight of *Monitor* vs. *Merrimac,* battles of Shiloh and Antietam. Homestead Act passed by Congress.
1864 Offenbach, on visit to Vienna, suggests that Johann write operettas.	1864 D.—Meyerbeer, Stephen Foster. B.—Richard Strauss.	1864 D.—Hawthorne. International Red Cross founded. Maximilian made Emperor of Mexico.
	1865 Première of Offenbach's *La Belle Hélène.*	1865 D.—Lincoln. B.—Kipling, George V. Civil War ends. Slavery abolished.
1866 Strauss writes *The Beautiful Blue Danube* for the Men's Singing Society.	1866 Moscow Conservatory opens. Prems. Smetana's *Bartered Bride,* Thomas' *Mignon,* Offenbach's *Barbe-Bleue* and *La Vie Parisienne.*	1866 Prussian war on Austria. Transatlantic cable finally laid. Invention of Whitehead torpedo, wood-pulp paper, electric dynamo. First nickel issued.
1867 In the spring Strauss goes to the Paris Exhibition to conduct, and then to Covent Garden, London.	1867 B.—Granados, Toscanini. Prems. of Offenbach's *La Grande Duchesse de Gerolstein,* Verdi's *Don Carlos,* Gounod's *Roméo et Juliette.* American prem. of Schubert's *Unfinished.*	1867 Maximilian of Mexico shot. B.—Mme. Curie, Wilbur Wright. U.S. purchase of Alaska. Lister describes antisepsis. Nobel invents dynamite. International Exhibition, Paris.
1868 Eduard Strauss promises to burn all of Josef's unpublished works on the latter's death.	1868 D.—Rossini. World prems. of *Die Meistersinger* by Wagner, Brahms's Waltzes, Op. 39, and Bruckner's 1st Symphony.	1868 D.—Kit Carson. President Johnson impeached, acquitted. Sholes patents the first typewriter. Cornell University is opened.

THE STRAUSS FAMILY	MUSICAL EVENTS	WORLD EVENTS
1870 Mother dies in February, Josef in July (but Eduard does not burn the music). Johann hears some of his experimental operetta music.	1870 B.—Oskar Straus, Lehar, Godowsky. Wagner marries Cosima Liszt. Premières of his *Walküre* and *Siegfried Idyll*.	1870 D.—Dickens, Dumas père, Lee, Farragut, B.—Lenin. Franco-Prussian War, and 3d French Republic. Kingdom of Italy estab. In U.S., Negroes are given the vote.
1871 His first operetta, *Indigo*, is produced on February 10.	1871 Royal Albert Hall opened, London. Prem. of Verdi's *Aida* at Cairo. The Damrosches come to the U.S.	1871 Stanley finds Livingstone in Africa. Chicago Fire. France capitulates, and German Empire is established.
1872 Goes to America, giving "mammoth" concerts in Boston and New York.	1872 Wagner starts building the Festival Theater at Bayreuth.	1872 D.—Greeley, Morse, Seward, Mazzini, Edwin Forrest. B.—Blériot, Amundsen.
1874 *Die Fledermaus* opens on April 5. His 30th anniversary is celebrated in Vienna.	1874 B.—Koussevitzky, Holst. Prem. of Mussorgsky's *Boris Godunov*. American prem. of Wagner's *Lohengrin*.	1874 B.—Churchill, Marconi. Boss Tweed convicted of fraud in N.Y.C. Charley Ross kidnaped, Philadelphia. Mississippi Bridge at St. Louis completed.
1878 Henrietta dies. He marries Angelika Diettrich, and is divorced from her after an unhappy marriage.	1878 N. Y. Symphony Orchestra founded by Leopold Damrosch. World première of Tchaikovsky's 4th Symphony.	1878 D.—Bryant. Edison patents the incandescent lamp. Salvation Army founded.
1880 *The Queen's Lace Handkerchief* is produced on October 1.	1880 D.—Offenbach, Wieniawski, Ole Bull.	1880 D.—Flaubert, George Eliot. B.—Helen Keller, Wilhelmina of the Netherlands.

1881 The Merry War is produced on November 25.	1881 D.—Mussorgsky. Boston Symphony founded. Prems. of Offenbach's *Tales of Hoffmann* and Gilbert and Sullivan's *Patience*.	1881 D.—Garfield, Disraeli. Ring Theater Fire, Vienna. Barnum and Bailey merge.
1883 Strauss marries Adele Deutsch.	1883 D.—Wagner. Prems. of Brahms's Symphony No. 3, Delibes' *Lakmé*. In N.Y.C., Metropolitan Opera opens.	1883 D.—Tom Thumb, Turgeniev. Brooklyn Bridge opened. Civil Service Reform Act passed.
1884 He celebrates the 40th anniversary of his debut as conductor.	1884 D.—Smetana. Prem. of Massenet's *Manon*. Russian Symphony Concerts open in St. Petersburg.	1884 D.—Wendell Phillips, Charles Reade. B.—Eduard Beneš. Fountain pen and linotype machine patented.
1885 The Gypsy Baron is produced on October 24.	1885 B.—Lotte Lehmann, Jerome Kern, Deems Taylor. Prems. of *The Mikado* and *Erminie*.	1885 D.—Grant, Victor Hugo. Cleveland inaugurated. In Baltimore, the first electric streetcars.
1894 His 50th anniversary as a conductor is recognized by gifts and congratulations from all over the world.	1894 D.—Bülow, Chabrier, Rubinstein. Prems. of Debussy's *Afternoon of a Faun*, Massenet's *Thaïs*.	1894 D.—Holmes, Stevenson, Kossuth. B.—Duke of Windsor. Strike and riots in Pullman, Ill. Coxey's Army marches to Washington.
1897 His last operetta, *The Goddess of Reason*, is produced on March 13.	1897 D.—Brahms. Prem. of Dukas' *The Sorcerer's Apprentice*.	1897 McKinley inaugurated. Andrée lost on balloon flight to North Pole.
1899 His final illness begins in May. He dies on June 3. Funeral on June 6.	1899 D.—Chausson. Prems. of Richard Strauss's *A Hero's Life*, Elgar's *Enigma Variations*.	1899 Marconi sends signals across Channel. U.S. war in Philippines. Boer War in South Africa.

GENERAL INDEX

(An index to the works of Johann Strauss, Jr., will be found on pages 215-16 following this General Index.)

General Index

INDEX TO THE WORKS OF
JOHANN STRAUSS, JR.

(*Note*—Numbers marked R indicate pages on which recordings are listed; marked M, pages on which the music is printed.)

215

I

D